Editor: Sarah Ratliff
Designer: Sanja Dzadzevic

Bleach on Colored Clothes

A Memoir

©2023 Joretta King

Boricua Digital

41 Avenida Fernando Luis Ribas

#449

Utuado, Puerto Rico 00641

boricuadigital.com

ISBN: 979-8-9872330-0-9 (Paperback)

ISBN: 979-8-9872330-1-6 (Hardcover)

ISBN: 979-8-9872330-2-3 (eBook)

First edition: January 2023

Disclaimer Notice

This book is a memoir. It reflects the author's recollections of experiences that took place over time. Some names and characteristics have been changed.

Notice of Liability

The information in this book is distributed on an "as is" basis, for informational purposes only, without warranty. While every precaution has been taken in the production of this book, neither the copyright owners nor the publisher shall have any liability to any person or entity with respect to any liability, loss, damage caused or alleged to be caused directly or indirectly by the information contained in this book.

Printed in the USA

Reviews of Bleach on Colored Clothes

As a native Hartsvillian and classmate of Joretta's, it would have been a natural instinct to become consumed with trying to determine the identity of each character. My heart ached for her as I read her truth of abandonment, homelessness and stolen innocence at the hands of adult men whom I probably crossed paths with daily.

Joretta captures the essence of the "Hero's Journey" in her jaw-dropping, irresistibly engaging memoir Bleach on Colored Clothes. She exposes the horrors and lasting effects of how being robbed of her innocence impacted every facet of her life. Her raw, transparent account of how her tranquil and loving childhood was disrupted by adversities that thrust her into an unimaginable lifecycle is tragic yet her resilience in the face of adversity is celebratory. Remarkably, amidst all of the drama and trauma, Joretta candidly shares her personal quest to encourage others to thrive in order to survive their personal adversities.

Joretta's style of writing is captivating. Her descriptive writing, creative use of dialect and diction gives life to each character. She takes you back to an era when South Hartsville's quaintness exhibited a sense of community. Her vivid depiction of the "juke joint" scene exposes grey areas of permissive behaviors she was introduced to at an early age. She openly shares aspects of what we have come to know culturally as the "generational curse." Her detailed account of being a victim of predatory behavior is mind-blowing.

Bleach on Colored Clothes was an awakening for me. It challenged my belief of my personal level of conscious awareness. I was not concerned with trying to figure out who A.C., Mr. D.J. or Mr. Billy were. Instead, it caused me to examine my level of consciousness. I repeatedly asked myself, "How did I go through elementary, high school and adulthood knowing nothing of Joretta's childhood, background or biological parentage? I was utterly bewildered by the fact I grew up in the same community totally oblivious to the cynicism that surrounded me.

I challenge my fellow Hartsvillians to read Bleach on Colored Clothes for personal insight, self-growth and as a call to action. Let us all strive to give true meaning to Dr. Maya Angelou's quote "Be a Rainbow in Someone Else's Cloud."

- Sharlene Wingate, former Hartsvillian, South Carolina

A book that you can't put down is a rarity, but Joretta King has written one. This is the story of a happy early childhood in rural South Carolina that spiraled downhill fueled by the continued abuse of her alcoholic parents. With each move, and there were many, we're taken into a realm of child and sexual abuse and hoping that this little girl could find a way out.

Joretta takes us through five decades of self-discovery. The road is never straight with continual ups and downs. She abused just like she was abused, with no excuses. She owns it all and learns from it all. She works on herself: mind, body and spirit. She leaves us in the present, and we can only hope that her future is brighter than her past and that she'll continue to write and share her world with us.

- Joan Kirchheimer, retired bed & breakfast owner, Puerto Rico

Bleach on Colored Clothes is a raw and authentic memoir that is simultaneously easy and difficult to read. It's easy because the story flows quickly, but difficult because you wonder what you'll read next illustrating what Ms. King has endured in her life. To those of us who grew up in traumatic, abusive situations, it is all too real, but it also reminds the reader to remain hopeful and keep striving for improvement. This is ultimately a story of her perseverance and finally, gratefully, truly learning self-love.

- Brandy Miller, Writer, California

Joretta King's Bleach on Colored Clothes will have you turning each page in anticipation. She tells her truth in full living color. Sometimes I read her agony with one hand over my mouth. I looked throughout her life for that one adult, just one who could have changed her path. Children shouldn't have to live the way she did. She fell through every crack there was and more. Joretta shows the reader a subculture and injustices that are sometimes hidden in plain sight.

I read the book twice because characters dropped in and out of Joretta's life and story, and I couldn't keep up. A second read only solidified my thoughts about those who failed her and her brother. While reading, I often thought and wondered about him. I hope she finds healing in the sharing of her story, and it provides a light toward an enlightened path.

- Lauren Johnson, Illinois

The minute everyday details shared by Joretta will draw you in and keep the pages turning in this honest and eye-opening retelling of her life. Joretta's experiences and choices throughout her life are shared in such an unforgiving way that you can't help but examine some of your own thoughts and beliefs.

- Ashley Thompson, Writer, Ontario

I really appreciate the opportunity given to me to read and review Bleach on Colored Clothes. From the first chapter, the description of the house and trees, I could see it vividly. Joretta's attention to detail brings this book to life.

The truth and rawness took me on an emotional ride from high to low, sad to mad, and hopeful to despair. It drew me in. It's engrossing in a way that you want to keep reading and want to know what happens next. That's what a good book will do, keep your attention.

The pace of the storytelling worked perfectly for me. I have read mysteries, thrillers, fantasies and autobiographical books. This book, I believe will do quite well if given the chance. Word of mouth will be the key because once I started reading it, I didn't want to stop.

- Edward Reed, Accounts Payable Manager, Georgia

I will begin by saying Wow!!! As I proceeded to read, I was entrenched by every description and explanation of events and circumstances. The magnitude of expression provided me with a precise understanding of each character. Joretta's ability to remain true and honest to her experiences has me personally examining my own bravery or lack thereof.

I want to thank Joretta for her courage and perseverance. This book will assist many people in their own journeys of self-actualization. I appreciate the opportunity to review such an intricate part of this triumphant human inwardness.

- Tambra Ketter-Tall, Owner, Salon Nu Breed, South Carolina

A thoroughly engaging and thought-provoking read, Bleach on Colored Clothes is a phenomenal story of hope, perseverance and the humbling depth of the human spirit.

Joretta's stories invoked sincere empathy for the shared, yet unique, forms of struggle and her profound resilience to just keep going. Heart-wrenching at times, Joretta's experiences embodied the potentially terrifying realities of inherited chaos and generational trauma, and how even in the most extreme cases, salvation can be found.

I was captivated by Joretta's journey, experiencing a roller coaster of emotions as her life story unfolded; it's humbling to realize that she actually lived through it all. I admire Joretta for having the courage to share her experiences, and I'm grateful for the opportunity to have learned about it through Bleach on Colored Clothes.

- Khalid Raoof, Entrepreneur, Puerto Rico

Let me first say thank you for trusting me to read such a riveting story. I appreciate the introduction that was provided. I believe it really set the stage for what was to come in the book. With that being said, this story was so good. I personally loved the way the story was laid out from beginning to end. It kept me engaged and even reminded me of some moments in my life when I didn't have it altogether but found the courage to get it together. Kudos on such a great book that I believe will encourage the masses in its own respective way.

- LaShawn McCray, M.S., Owner, The McCray Group, LL, Delaware

"Out of all the things I learned in school and church, nothing prepared me for a night on the streets in the middle of winter. I wandered aimlessly through the cold, dark, silent streets hoping someone would see me and Shawn and take us in. I prayed every prayer I knew, but no one came to our rescue..."

Bleach on Colored Clothes is a harrowing tale of abuse, survival, tenacity and redemption through self-knowledge, forgiveness, and self-love. Ms. King's childhood devolved from living in a two-parent sharecropping family to barely getting by in the city, into domestic violence, housing, food insecurity, sexual assaults, and sex work. Ms. King became "unmothered"/"unparented" as a result of the alcoholism, violence, and eventual separation of her parents, leaving Ms. King untethered to any type of support and vulnerable to sexual assault, bullying, and forced into sex work after being assaulted multiple times and not having a home.

Through the ups and downs of surviving a life in the streets, we see King's journey to rescue herself in fits and starts, with more than one attempt to return to school in hopes of improving her own life and that of her parents. We finally see her successfully gaining her GED as a single parent, despite so many of the adults and peers in her life constantly failing her and holding her in smallness and fear. We also observe repeating, and in some cases, escalating toxic patterns in her personal life, and that of her family, including getting thrown in jail for assault, unplanned pregnancies, abusing her children (verbally and physically), domestic violence and mental illness in her life and in the lives of her siblings. A lifelong determination for self-improvement leads to self-discovery, self-love, and bravery, which helps her forgive herself, forgive her mother and work to repair relationships with her children. I found myself wanting to cheer out loud by the end of the book, as it feels that Ms. King is on her way to the authentic and free life she has always wanted.

- Khalébo Harris, MBA, Training and Documentation Coordinator, New York

Bleach on Colored Clothes is the first book I've read in a long time that made me happy, sad, angry and every emotion in between at the same time. It almost reads like fiction, because at times it's hard to wrap your mind around the fact that all of these horrible things actually happened. But Joretta King rose like a phoenix from the ashes and wrote this beautiful, tragic memoir. Her voice and style of writing are unique and refreshing. Reading from her point of view, especially as a child, helps the reader experience all of the emotions King felt herself as if it were happening to them as well.

- Kristen Chandler, Editor and Writer, Alabama

In Loving Memory

Shawn Gregory King

(September 1966 to December 2020)

This book is dedicated to my Beloved brother Shawn Gregory King (aka Shawn-John Shawn-John).

I regret not writing this book sooner so you could be here to celebrate my story—or should I say, "our story," because this book is as much about you as it is about me. You always told me no one believed the things you told them you went through. I wished I could have done more to protect you. People would jokingly say that I was your mother and not your sister because of how dependent you were on me. My response was always, "He ain't heavy; he's, My brother."

What they didn't know I was equally dependent on you too. Dependent on your mental strength and sense of humor. Like the time I was going through something and called you crying hysterically. I didn't think I was going to be able to handle it and was ready to kill myself. You said, "Nah Jo, you can't go out like that. It's going to be all right. Plus, if you kill yourself, who's going to pay my phone bill?"

And I said, "F**K you, Shawn," and we both started laughing and I forgot all about harming myself. I miss calling you on Sundays and asking you what was going to happen on the Lifetime movie I was watching because I knew you had seen them all. When you came to Georgia and got a job at a restaurant and had everyone saying, "Lemme see yo whipstick!" But you never told them what that meant. Lol.

For those who may have judged, criticized, or condemned you because you may have zigged when you should have zagged, they didn't understand you were being a product of your environment. Shame on them for not getting to know how loving and caring you were. Your heart was as pure as the breath of a newborn baby. So, here's to you, "Shawn-John Shawn-John!" I hope I've made you proud. Your Big Sis Jo. I Love You Forever.

Foreword

I first met Joretta when she and I were part of a writing workshop. Joretta was one of several students and I served as their writing coach.

I had the honor of getting to know all the students through their writing. Given the caliber of writing all the women produced, I'm not surprised all of them would go on to complete their manuscripts and have them published. However, to be honest, Joretta's writing style, story and self-confidence, which she balanced with humility, stood out.

After reading excerpts of *Bleach on Colored Clothes*, I was moved to the point of tears, anger, and at times, elation. But there was another feeling I never shared with Joretta that would surprise her because she often refers to me as "the professional." Joretta is the definition of "the student surpasses the teacher."

When Joretta was nearing the completion of her manuscript, she approached me to see if I would be interested in editing and publishing *Bleach on Colored Clothes*. While I believe she did so with some trepidation, in truth, it was me who was intimidated. I read the manuscript in one night because I couldn't put it down. And judging from the reviews of *Bleach on Colored Clothes*, reactions have been the exact same.

Throughout the process of working on *Bleach on Colored Clothes*, I have enjoyed getting to know Joretta. While I don't want to overstep or overstate our relationship, I would like to believe we've become friends.

When Joretta asked me to write the foreword for *Bleach on Colored Clothes*, although flattered, I was immediately reluctant. In fact, I was completely against the idea. Why? I am not well-known in any field. I am not a scholar, a therapist or a trauma coach. If anything, I'm the antithesis of a "professional." I left my corporate job 15 years ago to live on an organic farm in the middle of the Atlantic Ocean. I use my years of experience to work with clients, like Joretta, whose projects bring me joy, versus working continuing to work on a career.

I'm a content writer with a few bylines, mainly in the cannabis industry. I've ghostwritten several books, in addition to the two books I've written and published - one about what it's like to be more than one race. Nothing

I've done to date is particularly noteworthy. I felt strongly Joretta needed someone with some credibility to explain why you should care about her memoir.

I looked around for *anyone* more qualified than me to write the foreword. And while I know many people with considerably more stature than I have, as I sat down to compose a request of someone to write a foreword for an author they'd never heard of, as I put words to paper, I realized something.

As the editor and publisher of *Bleach on Colored Clothes*, apart from Joretta, I have become the most intimate with her book. I haven't spent years writing the book in my head, eventually transferring those words to paper. I didn't start writing in my diary at the age of three, which would eventually serve as the first chapter of the book. What I have done is spend countless hours analyzing her book—from multiple angles: readability, clarity, how engaging it can be, and whether it can hold readers' attention. I have read it many times and become very familiar with it. And the more I read Joretta's words, the more attached to them I've become. You might say that I have become protective of both her memoir and Joretta.

But why? Why am I so moved by Joretta's story that I believe you will be as well? I'm not sure whether it's enough to say that I can relate. While I often win the battle of "who came from the most dysfunctional family?" and despite the seven years of therapy I required to overcome the trauma and abuse from being raised in a traumatic and violent home, my childhood, and its effect on my life as an adult don't hold a candle to what Joretta experienced.

Yes, I can relate to the trauma Joretta experienced as a child, particularly after her family left Ashland and moved to the town of Hartsville. The main difference between us is that I spent seven years on a therapist's couch talking about my trauma and abuse, as well as the generational trauma suffered on both sides of my family. Joretta didn't have this option. I will say how she overcame her childhood, while not conventional (and certainly not one I would recommend, as it often compounded the trauma she continually experienced as a child), was extremely effective—particularly when she started examining her life, the decisions she was making and ways to make major changes.

I hasten to make comparisons between new authors and established, even beloved authors. Still, after reading *Bleach on Colored Clothes*, I hope you'll forgive me this indulgence and perhaps even agree with me.

As a writer and editor, I am inspired by many authors from around the world. I am usually drawn to those who come from less-than-ideal homes for what I can only assume would be obvious reasons: relatability. The one constant theme in all the books I love reading–be they fiction or nonfiction–is that the protagonist is transformed for one reason or another.

Dr. Maya Angelou is one of my favorite authors. Her body of work is awe-inspiring, but two of her books speak to me and, in many ways, are what I was reminded of as I finished reading *Bleach on Colored Clothes*. For me, *Bleach on Colored Clothes* is what could have happened if Joretta had written about her life in two parts, which is how I see Dr. Angelou's I *Know Why the Caged Bird Sings* and *Wouldn't Take Nothing for My Journey Now*.

When Dr. Angelou wrote the former, she was deeply involved in the Civil Rights Movement. Writing her memoir wasn't something Angelou was even considering. At the same time, Angelou was playing an active role in the movement, she was enjoying life as a playwright, educator and poet and fielding offers from numerous places, including PBS.

Two satirical cartoonists, Jules and Judy Feiffer were so moved by Dr. Angelou's recounting of her childhood (both the story and the flair with which she told her story) they contacted the editor at Random House, Robert Loomis, who enlisted the help of James Baldwin to convince Angelou to write a memoir. *I Know Why the Caged Bird Sings* recounts Dr. Angelou's life until she turned 16. If you have read it, you know how powerful, sometimes harrowing and moving it is. If you haven't, I encourage you to do so.

Wouldn't Take Nothing for My Journey Now is, for me, Dr. Angelou at her most wise, the woman she became after baring her soul in *I Know Why the Caged Bird Sings* and walking her path. For me, *Bleach on Colored Clothes* is what happens when the younger Joretta meets the Joretta of today.

What do I mean, exactly?

Apart from the obvious: *I Know Why the Caged Bird Sings* and *Wouldn't Take Nothing for My Journey Now* are both about Dr. Angelou's life. Dr. Angelou's writing style evolved from one book to the other. As a writer, I can tell you this is both inevitable and welcomed. All writers look back on their prose from early on and will frequently pick apart everything that's wrong with it. The grammar and syntax weren't perfect, or more importantly, because anyone can improve on those two skills, what we wrote as "youngins" and the prose we wrote as we matured may bear little resemblance to one another.

You'll notice a few things as you read Joretta's *Bleach on Colored Clothes*— particularly the sections about her childhood. Joretta makes assumptions about your ability to catch on quickly—as well she should. She transitions from one theme to another and from referring to her parents as mommy and daddy to their first names, Bert and Howard, without so much as an explanation to you. If this seems or feels like something that might happen when talking with a child, you'd be right. Joretta began writing her memoir as a child sitting under the weeping willow tree in front of the home, where she spent the first few years of her life. The writing is less narrative than it is descriptive. Young Joretta tells her story as she saw it— from a child's perspective.

You'll also notice that, as the editor, I have chosen not to do much editing to Joretta's book. Except for editing for clarity, I have left Joretta's words intact because I feel you, as the reader, need to transform yourself into Joretta's world and take the journey as she experienced it from childhood to adulthood. I want you to live through her entire evolution—unfiltered and raw.

As Joretta's writing evolves, you'll see this transition as well, which coincides with her life shifting and changing. I believe Joretta has a unique style of writing that was already evident when she was a child.

In my opinion, an editor's job is to leave the writer's words as authentic as possible. So, for me, making "corrections" that are more in line with "proper" grammar, syntax and punctuation would serve only one purpose: to appease strict grammarians. It does absolutely nothing for the story, and if anything, doing so would detract from Joretta's brilliant prose.

As a reader about to walk in Joretta's shoes, all I ask is for you to keep a completely open mind. Don't judge. Don't assume, don't overthink it, and please don't filter. Just go with it. Just allow Joretta's prose to guide you through her journey. I will give you a spoiler alert. Joretta didn't use very conventional or traditional means to break the cycle of generational trauma. For my feelings on that, I again turn to Dr. Maya Angelou not once, but twice: "If you're always trying to be normal, you will never know how amazing you can be" and "You may kill me with hatefulness, but still like air, I rise."

To quote one of my favorite musicians, the late George Michael, "Listen without prejudice."

Sarah Ratliff

Table of Contents

INTRODUCTION

I Stood Yesterday. I Can Stand Today

- Dorothy Dix

--- - Bleach on Colored Clothes - ---

When I look back on the totality of my life, I am often drawn to the words of suffragist, journalist and advice columnist Dorothy Dix, née Elizabeth Meriwether (November 18, 1861 – December 16, 1951).

I have been through the depths of poverty and sickness. When people ask me what has kept me going through the troubles that come to all of us, I always reply, "I stood yesterday. I can stand today. And I will not permit myself to think about what might happen tomorrow."

I have known want and struggle and anxiety and despair. I have always had to work beyond the limit of my strength. As I look back upon my life, I see it as a battlefield strewn with the wrecks of dead dreams, and broken hopes and shattered illusions—a battle in which I always fought with the odds tremendously against me, and which has left me scarred, and bruised and maimed, and old before my time.

Yet, I have no pity for myself; no tears to shed over the past and gone sorrows; no envy for the women who have been spared all I have gone through. For I have lived. They only existed. I have drunk the cup of life down to its very dregs. They have only sipped the bubbles on top of it.

I know things they will never know. I see things to which they are blind. It is only the women whose eyes have been washed clear with tears who get the broad vision that makes them little sisters to all the world. I have learned in the great University of Hard Knocks a philosophy that no woman who has had an easy life ever acquires. I have learned to live each day as it comes and not to borrow trouble by dreading the morrow. It is the dark menace of the picture that makes cowards of us.

I put that dread from me because experience has taught me that when the time comes that I so fear, the strength and wisdom to meet it will be given me. Little annoyances no longer have the power to affect me.

After you have seen your whole edifice of happiness topple and crash in ruins about you, it never matters to you again that a servant forgets to put the doilies under the finger bowls, or the cook spills the soup. I have learned not to expect too much of people, and so I can still get happiness out of the friend who isn't quite true to me or the acquaintance who gossips. Above all, I have acquired a sense of humor, because there were so many things over which I had to either cry or laugh. And when a woman can joke over her troubles instead of having hysterics, nothing can ever hurt her much again.

I do not regret the hardships I have known, because through them, I have touched life at every point I have lived, and it was worth the price I had to pay.

As you read the words of my life story, I'd like you to keep something in mind. I wrote *Bleach on Colored Clothes* at various points in my life. Initially, it began with writing in my diary as a child, taking note of things children observe. Over time as I had to learn to work through the struggles you will read about, writing was a way to keep me sane. As I matured and set out on the journey to heal myself and become who I am today, I finished writing my story.

As you can imagine, my writing style has evolved, along with my understanding of the mechanics of writing. When I gave my manuscript to my editor, we talked over whether I should have her "polish" my prose so from the first word to the last, it read as though I came out of my mother's womb with perfect grammar, sentence structure and punctuation.

Nothing is further from the truth. My editor feels she was handed a gift. It's not often an editor gets a manuscript that was written over the course of one's life, enabling the reader to see how the author's life and writing evolved. Most memoirs are written with a retrospective view. It's difficult to revert to the earlier versions of one's writing style, and so most memoirs are polished because they're written almost entirely from the perspective of an adult.

Bleach on Colored Clothes is different in that I want to take on the entire journey, which includes an unfiltered and raw look at who I was and whom I have evolved into. Apart from editing for clarity (to avoid confusion), my editor and I have decided to do something not often seen in memoirs: leave my words entirely intact. As you read my story, our hope is you will see the entire evolution: not just my healing, but how my writing has changed, which keeps pace with my story as it unfolds.

As my editor notes in the final words of her foreword, in the words of the late George Michael, "Listen without prejudice."

CHAPTER 1

The tragedy of life is what dies inside a man while he lives.

- Dr. Albert Schweitzer

- Bleach on Colored Clothes -

I heard the glass shatter, then Bert screaming and crying, "Oh Lord Jesus! NOOOO!!!!" It was April 4, 1968. It was just announced on the radio that Dr. Martin Luther King Jr. was assassinated. People came to the house to see if Bert knew because we didn't have a television and they wanted to see if she was okay. They all stood around in the kitchen crying and consoling one another. I was four years old and didn't fully understand who he was. All I knew was that his picture was on the wall in our living room with all the other family photos. And because his last name was King, I thought he was related to me.

The weeks following his death wasn't the same. I saw Bert crying often and saying under her breath, "Lord, what we gon do now?" We didn't go out in the cotton field as often. A lot of the cotton pickers also stopped coming.

This would be my last time living in the cinder block house and sitting under the willow tree. The next month we packed up and moved to Hartsville.

Hartsville is a small town in South Carolina with a population of around 7,000 founded in 1891 by a plantation owner named James Hart. About twelve miles outside of Hartsville is a smaller town called Ashland (current population is 3,500). I spent the first four years of my life in Ashland.

My earliest memories are from when I was three years old. I was a happy, vibrant and inquisitive three-year-old girl who paid attention to everything around me. The house we lived in was built with cinder blocks and sat way back off a long dirt road. It had a living room also called the front room, a kitchen and two bedrooms: one for my parents and the other one for the children.

There was a weeping willow tree in the front yard and a pecan tree on the side. Directly in front of the house were fields of cotton that stretched for miles and miles. My mommy stayed home with the children while my daddy worked. There were seven of us. I was the youngest of four girls and my brother Shawn was the baby. The three oldest were from a previous relationship. They lived with my maternal grandmother and four of us lived with my mommy and daddy.

My mommy was a petite lady who stood about 5'5" and weighed about 130 lbs. She had smooth dark chocolate skin, small round eyes, straight white teeth and full lips. She had short fine hair that barely touched the top of her ears. The biggest thing on her was her big, beautiful, toned legs. In the summer she always wore shorts, dresses or skirts. She was always busy doing something: cooking, cleaning or doing laundry. I hardly ever saw her sitting down. She was the first one to get up in the morning and the last one to go to bed at night. One of my favorite things to do was help her hang the clothes on the line to dry. I trailed behind her holding the small tin pan filled with clothes pins, handing her one at a time as she hung the clothes in their respective category. Once all the clothes were on the line, it was on to the next chore. Everything she did was scheduled. Breakfast, lunch and dinner was the exact same time every day. Meals were always planned and prepared in advance. Chicken and pork chops were cleaned the morning of and seasoned with Lawry's' seasoned salt, table salt and black pepper. Fresh greens and peas were served with every meal.

Every Saturday morning Mr. Pooler (I called him the vegetable man) drove right up to the front door in an old rickety black truck loaded with fresh vegetables. Bert carefully inspected the stalks of collard greens, mustard and turnip greens before buying them. She then grabbed handfuls of black-eyed peas and lima beans, put them in a brown paper bag and gave Mr. Pooler the money. "See ya next Saturday," he said. With a half-smile, she replied, "Okay, Thank you."

Bert was very soft-spoken and said very little. One day when she was in the kitchen, I heard her mumble, "these some pretty collards. I shoulda got some corn on the cob." I sat at the kitchen table watching her every move. After removing the big red rubber band later used for my ponytail and to keep Jean's socks from falling) that held the collards together, she cut the stalks off and washed the leaves, submerging them into the water as if they were being baptized. After removing them from the water, she wiped them down with a cloth, rolled three to four leaves together, sliced them into skinny ribbons and rinsed them three more times before cooking. Soon as the greens started cooking, she took the pieces of seasoned chicken, tossed them in a brown paper bag with flour and shook 'em up before dropping them in a pan of hot grease. Between stirring the collards and turning the chicken, she mixed the cornbread, slid it in the oven and put on a pot of rice. She made cooking look like a choreographed dance routine.

I heard my daddy's footsteps and ran towards him. He always made it home just in time for dinner and I was always excited to see him, even more excited about what he brought me. "Hey Baby Girl!" he'd always say as he picked me up and put me back down. I stood there not saying a word, looked up at him with my tiny hands opened, with a look on my face that said, *"give it up!"* He reached in his pocket and handed over a chocolate moon pie, then he was free to go. My daddy was a big light-skinned man about 6'4 and weighed about 240 lbs. He had huge hands and wore a size 15 shoe. He was very handsome, with big, beautiful eyes and a captivating smile. He always kept his hair cut and his mustache trimmed. I looked a lot like my daddy. I had his eyes, nose, and smile, and a creamy caramel complexion that was a perfect blend of his and my mommy.

A plate full of Bert's delicious food awaited him at the table: golden fried chicken, collard greens, lima beans, rice, cornbread, and a tall glass of sweetened iced tea with perfectly sliced lemons.

She sat at the table and ate with him, which is one of the rare times she sat down. Their conversation was mainly about what was going on with other people, but she also enjoyed watching him eat. She knew he loved her cooking, and his lip-smacking, finger-licking and plate-licking confirmed it. Once my daddy finished eating it was our turn. We sat at the yellow metal table with two hollow matching chairs that when moved over the concrete floor, made an annoying, scraping sound.

Bert saved the wishbone for me from the piece of chicken my daddy had eaten. I closed my eyes and wished for a new doll for Christmas. After dinner, she cleaned the kitchen and brought the clothes in off the line. After folding the clothes, it was time for our bath. She filled the big round tin tub with warm water, and my sister Jean and I got in. I was always fascinated by the floating bar of soap I thought I could make stay at the bottom of the tub, but as soon as I moved my hand, it floated right back to the top.

She took me and Jean out of the tub, dried us off and greased us down with Vaseline˚ before putting our nightgowns on. She put my brothers in the tub and added more warm water to the same water Jean and I bathed in. The girls always got to go first because she said the boys were dirtier than girls. Bert made sure we said our prayers every night before going to bed. She kneeled beside me, and I repeated after her; "*Now I lay me down to sleep. I pray the Lord my soul to keep. If I should die before I wake, I pray the Lord my soul to take. Amen.*" After putting us to bed, I could still hear her moving around in the kitchen: washing the dishes and mopping the floor, fumigating the house with bleach and Pine-Sol˚.

The next morning at the crack of dawn she was up. My daddy had already left for work and my sister Jean and brother Wade had left for school. She wiped my face and hands with a warm cloth and sat me at the table. There were two strips of bacon, grits, scrambled eggs, and a piece of toast with a smiley face made with a pad of butter at the top left and right corner, one in the middle and three at the bottom, topped with a teaspoon of grape jam. While I ate my breakfast, she drank a cup of coffee. Her favorite was Folgers˚ with equal amounts of cream and sugar. She listened intently to the voice of Paul Harvey coming from the tiny radio that sat in the windowsill. Every so often nodding her head in agreement with what he was saying, sipping her coffee from the white porcelain cup and placing it on the matching saucer.

"Come on Jo and get dressed. We gotta go out in the field." With my brother Shawn tied to her back, I held onto her dress with one hand and a shoebox with the other. There were other men, women and children in the field picking cotton. The women and children picked from one side while the men picked from the other. As Bert filled the burlap sacks with cotton, I filled my shoebox. Hours passed before we took a break and then it was only to get a drink of water. The sun had no mercy on us. Bert picked cotton with one hand while constantly wiping the sweat from her forehead with the other. I trailed behind her, my tiny feet disappearing in the hot soil.

Once her sacks were filled, we made our way back to the house. As we got closer, there was a white man sitting in a truck under the willow tree. One at a time, the people took their cotton and dumped it in a sheet. The man placed it on a scale and handed them some money. When it was our turn, I gave him my shoebox. He gave me a nickel and gave Bert some money. Once in the house, we all washed up and she started dinner. She gave me a piece of watermelon and I sat under the weeping willow tree trying to eat it as fast as I could before the gnats and flies did.

"I'm finna do yo' hair, cause we going to town tomorrow." She put two pillows on the floor, and I sat between her legs. "I want three ponytails," I told her. She scooped out a big hunk of Royal Crown* hair grease, placed it on the back of her hand and greased my scalp. Sectioning my hair into three parts, I handed her the big red rubber bands: two for the front and one for the back. Going to town was a big deal. It was a chance for everyone to dress up. Bert wore her nice dress and sandals, curly short wig, red lipstick, and fancy pocketbook on her shoulder. Howard had on his khaki pants with a white shirt tucked inside, and a brown belt to match his brown loafers. All the children had on short sets and Buster Brown* shoes. It was also exciting to see other people because living way out in the country was like living in our own little world. The only people we saw were the cotton pickers and the vegetable man.

Mr. D.J. picked us up in his gold Chevrolet. Howard sat in the front and Bert sat in the back seat with Shawn, Jean and Wade. I sat on my daddy's lap with my face towards the window the entire time admiring the trees, blue sky and other cars passing by. The drive to Hartsville seemed far away. My eyes lit up with excitement when Mr. D.J. pulled in front of Eli's Candy Kitchen. This place was a child's dream come true. There were all sorts of candy, cookies, popcorn and treats to choose from. I filled my bag with

Squirrel Nut Candy* and Mary Janes*. The place was always packed with people. Bert stopped and talked with people she knew, or some would just pass by and say, "Dem some fine chillun you got there," and keep walking.

From there we went to the Army Navy store, which really wasn't my favorite because there wasn't anything in there for little girls. Bert and Howard shopped there for Army coats and wool blankets in preparation for the brutal winter. The only heat we had was a wooden stove, and once the fire went out, it was so cold you could see your breath.

Before going back home, we stopped by my grandmother Kate's house. Everybody called her "Mama." Mama lived in a white wooden house with a big front porch and a huge backyard. She was a petite frail lady with golden bronze skin and wore her silky silver hair in two big plaits. Her eyes so crystal clear, looking into them was like looking at clear water. She was the sweetest lady I'd ever seen. Most of her time was spent on the front porch in her rocking chair, reading her Bible. "Hey mama," Bert greeted her with a big smile. "Hey Bert!" she said while giving all of us a hug. Then we ran in the house to see the other siblings. My brother Smoky was in the room playing his guitar. He got his nickname Smoky because he was so dark. He was about 5'9", medium build, and when he walked, he dragged his feet. Most of the time he stayed to himself, and you could always find him picking his guitar or drawing.

My sisters Gail and Linda were hanging out in the backyard. As soon as Linda saw Jean, she started chasing her around the house trying to bite her. I'm not sure why, but she loved biting her and no one else. While Linda continued to chase Jean, the rest of us played. Gail and Wade played kickball, and I ran through Mama's sheets on the clothesline. Shawn stayed on the porch with Bert and Mama while Howard and Mr. D.J. stayed in the car and talked.

"Y'all, come on in the house and eat ya supper!" Mama yelled. We all gathered at the table for Mama's neckbones and rice, fatback, collard greens and hot homemade biscuits dipped in cane patch syrup. After dinner, we said our goodbyes and headed back to the country.

Following Dr. King's assassination, the move to Hartsville was bittersweet. While I missed the old house, the cotton field, and the weeping willow tree, I liked seeing other people and having children to play with. Hartsville was a friendly town where you were always greeted with a nod and a smile. Everyone in Hartsville knew everyone and *their* business. It was like one big family. We moved to an area called, "Hop-Town." As to how it got its name, I'm not sure. Some said it was named after a gang called, "The Hop-Town Boys." Others said that's where all the *happenings* were. It was a modest three-room house with two large rooms and a kitchen. One room was a living room/bedroom and the other one was Bert and Howard's bedroom. There were two big beds next to the windows on the right side of the room, one for the girls and one for the boys. A brown stereo and sofa on the left side, and the dresser in the corner. Two streets over were a small community of nicer homes where some of the teachers lived who taught at the historically Black high school adjacent from our house. Directly across the street was "The Big M" convenient store. By the time we moved to Hartsville, Linda was about to graduate from high school, Gail was a sophomore, Smoky was a junior, Jean and Wade were in elementary school, and I would start kindergarten in the fall.

The neighbor to our left was a beautiful older woman who looked to be well into her 60s. I referred to her as the "Indian lady" because she had high cheekbones, dark almond-shaped eyes and reddish-brown skin. Her granddaughter Grace and grandson Verne lived with her.

It wasn't long before we were all outside playing. Bert continued her same routine: cooking, cleaning and washing clothes. She also seemed a little more at ease. Maybe because she had a television to watch her soap operas or "stories," as she called them. *Search for Tomorrow, Guiding Light and As the World Turns* were her favorites. She also had a telephone to call her friends and talk about what happened on the stories. With all Bert had to do, she still managed to keep an eye on us while we were outside. Our kitchen window faced Grace and Verne's house and we had to play in the middle. If we went a few feet out of her view, she'd yell, "Y'all need to get back over here where I can see y'all!" We didn't have toys to play with yet were never bored. We entertained ourselves by playing Hopscotch, Ring Around the Rosie and The Hokey Pokey.

Grace and Verne's grandmother's yard was off-limits. It was well-manicured with beautiful bushes of blue, purple and green hydrangeas. One day I ran over to get one and just as I was about to pick it, I heard a voice say, "I beg your pardon?" She was looking out of her bedroom window. I took off running as fast as I could, but I was determined to get a flower for Bert.

The second time she caught me, she said, "I beg your pardon?" On my third attempt I had the flower in my hand and before I could take one step, "I beg your pardon?" I looked at her and said, "I beg your pardon?" and ran! "Thank you, Jo," Bert said, smiling as I handed her the flower. "Did you ask Ms. Partner if you could have it?" I shook my head no. Bert told me this was considered stealing, and I needed to apologize. We walked over to Ms. Partner's house "Sorry for taking your flower, Ms. Pardon." *Partner* sounded like *Pardon* to me, and from that day forward Ms. Pardon is what I called her.

It was Saturday morning and both sides of the street were packed with men, women and children lined up to see the high school's annual homecoming parade. It would be my first time seeing it. First came the majorettes twirling their batons—Gail right in front. My eyes followed her every move as she threw the baton up in the air, catching it and twirling it behind her back. Next were the cheerleaders with their purple and gold pom poms. But it was when the band played, "The Horse" that made the crowd go wild. As the parade marched passed the crowd, some of the older children followed alongside the band, every step of the way.

After the parade, Bert made Howard's lunch. "We finna walked down to mama's house." Howard had already gotten comfortable with his khaki pants and white tank t-shirt. Saturday was his day to stay home and watch television. Bert handed him a plate of fried bologna sandwiches with pork n beans. "Gimme a beer out da Kelvinator™ [1]" He pulled back the tab on the Pabst Blue Ribbon`, took a sip, "Aah! it's good and cold." He would sit in front of the TV for hours laughing at Festus on *Gunsmoke* and Hoss on *Bonanza*.

A little sweet old lady named Mrs. Pearl lived next door to mama. She was short, brown-skinned, with silver hair. You could tell she was a beautiful woman in her younger years as she still wore her golden years very well. Her house was white with a beautiful yard, surrounded by a chain link fence. She owned a little red candy store that was connected to her house.

---

[1] The Kelvinator Corporation, a pioneer in automatic refrigeration technology, had its roots in 1914 with Buick executives Edmund J. Copeland and Arnold H. Goss.
https://detroithistorical.org/learn/encyclopedia-of-detroit/kelvinator-corporation

If she wasn't inside the store, all we had to do was stand in the middle of the street and Yell, "Mrs. Pearl!!!!!" And she'd come walking out slowly and open the store knowing we only had fifty cents each to spend. "Why is Linda walking around with that coat on as hot as it is?" Bert asked Mama.

"I dun know," Mama said. "She probably ain't got no blood." I knew when Pat didn't chase Jean around the house trying to bite her, something had to be wrong.

We got back home just before dark, and Howard was still right where we left him in front of the TV with about five empty beer cans around him. Bert fixed supper and got us ready for bed. From the corner of my eye, I saw Bert grease her legs and feet with Vaseline™. She slipped her mini dress on top of her slip and massaged Pond's˙ cream on her face. She dabbed the red rubber sponge in her face powder and rubbed it on her face. Applied her red lipstick, took her long wig off the mannequin's head and placed it on her head on top of the stocking cap. She put on her earbobs, necklace and shoes. She took the powder puff out of the cashmere bouquet powder and dusted her cleavage, and out the door she went. *Where was she and Howard going this time of night?* I asked myself. They couldn't be going very far because they didn't have a car and neither one of them knew how to drive.

A few minutes later, I heard loud voices of men and women laughing and talking. It sounded like it was coming from next door to the right of us, but no one lived there. Suddenly, I heard "Having a Party" by Sam Cooke. "Ahh!!! Shu Now!" "Get it Bert!" I could hear the ladies shouting. I didn't know who all was talking, just heard ladies' voices.

"Jean! Jean! Do you hear that?" I asked my sister.

"Hear what?" Jean replied.

"The noise coming from next door." I replied.

"Oh, the juke joint? That's where grown folks go and have fun. You better go to sleep," Jean said.

Bert started working next door cleaning up on the weekends. She picked up beer cans, and bottles, emptied ashtrays and swept the floor. Jean and I ran around picking up change off the floor. Bert gave us a handful of quarters to play the piccolo. "Mash numbers A24, B19, C12 and D6 three times," Bert instructed Jean and me.

After hearing Percy Sledge, Wilson Pickett, and Otis Redding, we'd have to listen to, "Can I Change My Mind?" by Tyrone Davis again and again.

Howard came barging through the door with the biggest Christmas tree I'd ever seen. It was the weekend after Thanksgiving and the tradition was to put up the tree and decorations. Bert strung the tree with lights and Howard hung the lights around the outside of the house. Jean helped place the red and gold Christmas ball ornaments and icicles, and I added the candy canes. Bert cleared off the top of the stereo that was used as the television stand. She pulled out the Christmas albums and from that day until New Year's Day, all we listened to were, "Please Come Home for Christmas" by Charles Brown, "Merry Christmas Baby" by Otis Redding and "Gee Whiz, It's Christmas" by Carla Thomas. The weeks leading up to Christmas was spent going to the store shopping for food and other household items. Bert also helped with writing our Christmas list. She'd remind us, "Make sure you're good and Santa will give you anything you ask for." All I wanted for Christmas was that bright yellow Easy-Bake Oven and a SWINGY doll.

Different people came by with baskets of fruits and a variety of nuts. There was one nut we weren't allowed to eat. I asked Bert why.

"Oh, that's a nigger toe." She replied.

With a perplexed look, I asked her, "What's a nigger toe?"

"White folks call it a nigger toe 'cause they say it looks like Black people toes, so we don't eat those."

It was Christmas Eve and Bert started preparing her dinner early in the morning. For Christmas dinner, Bert also made her most requested upside-down pineapple cake and she would always let me lick the spoon. Later that evening after dinner she got us dress for bed and told us, "Make sure you all go to sleep because you know Santa Claus will not leave presents for little children who are awake. If you're awake, he will put black pepper in your eyes." I was so excited but afraid at the same time because I did not want Santa Claus to put pepper in my eyes. I closed my eyes tight and took one last peek out the window. The sky was clear, and the stars were so bright. It felt like Santa Claus was on his way and I just thought maybe I could possibly see Santa Claus on his sleigh with Rudolph leading the way.

Christmas morning, all our presents were under the tree. I ripped the paper off my presents and there was my Easy-Bake˚ Oven and a SWINGY doll! After playing with my toys, Bert took us outside so we could make a snowman. Later that day, she made homemade ice cream from the snow. It was the best ice cream I'd ever tasted. I was amazed at how creative she was with cooking. She could take something so simple and turn it into something so amazing.

The New Year's Day tradition was for a man to walk through the house before anybody came in or else it was considered bad luck for the rest of the year. Mr. D.J. usually came by, but he wasn't available, so Howard had to get up early and walk through every room in the house, leave out the back door and then come back in through the front door. Then Bert could start cooking the good luck meal of black-eyed peas, collard greens and fried chicken.

Howard jumped up and ran to the door to see what the loud banging was. Smoky ran in screaming, "Linda! Linda's going to the hospital! Her stomach is hurting. We think she swallowed a watermelon seed!" When Bert saw her with that coat on in 90-degree weather, she was wondering why. It was because she was trying to hide her baby. When we were younger the older people would tell us, "When y'all eat that watermelon, make sure you spit dem seeds out cause if you swallow em', they'll grow in your stomach, and you'll have a watermelon baby." Later that night, Linda gave birth to a baby boy.

It was about seven months after Linda had her baby that Smoky came busting through the door again late one night. He was drenched in sweat yelling and screaming. "Mama... Mama... Mama!!!"

"What's wrong wit you, boy!?" Bert yelled at Smoky. He was out of breath and could barely speak.

"Mama! she's ... she's ... DEAD!!!"

"LAWD JESUS! what you talkin' bout boy!" Bert tried to get Smoky to calm down and make sense.

"I saw her on her knees praying and after she didn't git up, I thought maybe she fell asleep. I picked her up and put her in the bed. Her body was still warm. I went back to check on her and she was stiff as a board."

Bert hurriedly put on some clothes, and they ran down to Mama's house. And sure, enough Mama was gone. After Mama's funeral, Linda took her baby and Gail, and moved to New York. Smoky moved in with us. And for whatever reason, Wade went to live with Howard's mother Eunetha. Everyone called her Neat, so I called her Grandma Neat.

It was Saturday afternoon. We were sitting on the couch watching cartoons, Howard came in the house all excited. "Y'all come out here and looka what I gotcha." We jumped up, ran outside, and standing there was a big beautiful black and white dog with long straight hair. "Where did you get this dog from? Is it a boy or a girl?" Howard never answered, nor did he know its name. Jean and I debated over whether to name it Lassie after the popular female dog TV show or Fluffy. After finding out it was a boy, Fluffy was more appropriate. Fluffy adapted right away and we fell in love with him. Even Bert didn't seem to be as sad about Mama's passing.

Fluffy became everything we all needed. We couldn't have asked for a better dog. He stayed in the backyard and barked whenever he heard or saw something and ate whatever scraps we fed him. Our school was several blocks away. On the days Bert couldn't walk us to school, Fluffy did. And he would be right there waiting for us when school was out.

Now that Linda, Gail and Wade were gone, I had to start doing chores. After dinner, the dishes had to be washed, dried and put away. The floors had to be swept and mopped. I didn't mind doing any of it, but the one thing I despised the most was having to empty the piss pot.

It was a round white ceramic pot with a red handle and white lid, trimmed in red. It was our portable potty because we didn't have indoor plumbing. There was an old wooden shed (the outhouse) in the backyard. I wasn't old enough to go to the outhouse by myself, so Bert had to take me. It was old, dark and stinky from everybody's waste.

Bert and Howard started going to the juke joint next door more frequently. One night after they came home, I heard what sounded like arguing:

"You tellin' a damn lie!" Howard yelled at Bert.

"See there you go. You be alright 'til you git that liquor in you, then you start acking a fool!" Bert shot back.

"You might thank imma fool, but I ain't no fool. I know what I seent!" Howard explained.

"Lord, Howard, that man wasn't paying me no attention." Bert tried to convince Howard, but he wasn't having none of it.

The tone of Howard's voice scared me. This was the first time I'd ever heard them argue. I could feel my heart beating faster, afraid of what was going to happen. Not knowing what to do, I felt like I needed to let him know I wasn't asleep and heard everything he said. I loved my daddy, and I knew he loved me. But I loved my mommy even more and I was willing to protect her any way I could. I got up and walked in their room and stood in the doorway. "Baby girl, you alright?" Howard asked me.

"You scare me, Howard! You scare me!" I was trying to compose myself, but it wasn't easy.

"Aww, we ain't doin nuthin, but playin" he said with a grin.

And to reassure me Bert laughed too. I went back to bed as I was told, knowing there was more to it than what they were telling me.

The next morning was as if nothing ever happened. Howard ate his breakfast and was on his way out the door. "You need me to git anythang from da sto' dis evening?" he asked Bert. "Yeah, I need some milk to make the cornbread. "Oh, and git a small bag of grits and two cans of potted meat."

Howard never made it back home that night or the next day. Bert didn't seem to be too worried about it. If so, she didn't let it show. It was as if she knew he wasn't hurt or in any trouble. Two days later, Howard came home with no milk, grits, potted meat or explanation. He sat down in his favorite chair and took his shoes off. "Go fix me a plate" he ordered Bert.

Without saying a word, Bert walked in the kitchen. Shawn and I followed. She mumbled under her breath, "I'll fix you something to eat alright." I noticed she didn't get any food from the pots on the stove. I saw her pour water in a container and stir it up.

"Can we have some of what you making?" Shawn asked Bert.

"No, this here for yo' daddy. Y'all move out da way." She wrapped a dishcloth around the container, walked in the room and SWOOSH! She threw the liquid right in Howard's face.

"GOD DAMMIT!!!!" Howard was screaming holding his face and ran straight through the screen door knocking it off the hinges.

Smoky was screaming and crying. "Oh my God! Oh my God!" Bert didn't realize the liquid she threw on Howard splashed onto Smoky's face. She ran and got the piss pot and dashed the piss in his face to stop the burning.

The chair Howard was sitting in was right in front of the bed where Smoky was. I saw on the container, RED DEVIL LYE. A few hours later, the police brought Howard home, his face all bandaged. "Mrs. King, can I talk to you for a minute? I was called to the emergency room. Your husband's face is burned very badly. He said you threw lye on him. Do you realize you could've blinded him? I should take you to jail, but your husband asked me not to."

I could see how frightened Bert was. She stood there not saying a word, looking at the officer as if she was being scolded by a parent. The policeman left and Howard didn't say one word the rest of the night.

Shortly thereafter, Smoky was drafted into the Army, leaving me, Shawn and Jean. For a while, things seemed to go back to normal. Howard even started cooking and gave Bert a break.

One night I opened the refrigerator to get something to drink and there was a huge hog's head in the refrigerator staring right at me! Howard was a hunter, and he always came home with some kind of animal; raccoon, he referred to as coon, rabbits and chickens, but I didn't expect to see the whole head of a hog. Out of the hog's head, Howard made the best hog head cheese, pig ears and fried pork skins. On Fridays, he brought us a special treat: a cold bottle of Pepsi-Cola and a pack of salted peanuts. We'd take a couple of drinks, pour the peanuts in the bottle, and drank and eat them at the same time. After all the soda was gone, we'd hit the bottom of the bottle to get the peanuts that sank to the bottom.

Later that evening, Howard and Bert went to the juke joint like they always did. It was a little past 8:30 and Jean and I were sitting on the couch watching *Green Acres*. Shawn was on the floor playing with his G.I. Joe action figures. Howard ran in the house, "Baby!!!! he called out to Shawn. C'mere, Lemme sho you sumthin."

Shawn followed Howard into the kitchen. Howard took a gun out of his pocket and put in the oven. "The police finna take me wit dem. As soon as I leave, I want you to git da gun out da oven and bury it in the backyard. You herr me?" Shawn stood there trembling, shaking his head "okay." With tears streaming down our faces, we watched as the police handcuffed Howard and put him in the back of the car and took him away.

Every time Bert and Howard went to the juke joint, a man named Sabbath kept flirting with her. Howard accused him and Bert of messing around. That night they got into an argument and Howard shot him. Sabbath died on the way to the hospital. Months later it was rumored it wasn't the gunshot Howard fired that killed Sabbath, but the white emergency service men who took him in da ambalamps.

Bert's friend told her what happened which was all hearsay: "You know dey say Sabbath had kilt one of them Skinner boys years ago and ran off to New York City." Bert's friend said.

"And Dem Skinner boys been looking for him ever since. When dey saw it was Sabbath, dey said, 'this the Nigger we been looking for.'" Bert's friend told her.

"I wondered why they been comin' round heh lately." Her friend said.

"I been seeing em' over at da Big M looking this a way."

Bert's friend told her the story as if she were an eyewitness.

"Knowing them, they probably did kill Sabbath. They ain't nuthin but some ole Po'buckers[2]." Bert continued.

It was the opinion of the people who were at the juke joint believed Sabbath could've possibly survived the gunshot, but The Skinners killed him on the way to the hospital. Whether or not it was true, Howard was charged and sentenced to three years of hard labor on the Chain Gang.

As if Bert didn't have enough to do already, she was now left with the responsibility of everything now that Howard was gone. I watched her cut huge logs of wood in the freezing cold, chopping away at it tirelessly with so much force and determination, refusing to give in, knowing it would break before she did. Once she had it all cut up, I was right to help her carry it in, piece by piece. She made a fire in the wood-burning stove to heat the house and water for our baths, and to cook our meals when the lights were turned off.

---

[2] Po'bucker is slang used primarily in the Deep South by Black people to describe who they considered to be the devil, a.k.a. the white man. It is believed to have been derived from the word Bukker, brought to the new world by enslaved people from West Africa.

"Y'all c'mon in this house. It's a big dark cloud." The rain was violent, mixed with explosive thunder and crackling lightning.

"Y'all sit down and be quiet." Bert unplugged the TV and everything else, pulled all the shades, and covered the mirrors with blankets.

"Ouch!" I yelled.

"Didn't I tell y'all to sit still and be quiet while the Lord doing his work?" Bert scolded.

"Jean pinched me!"

"No, I didn't" Jean said.

"Yes, you did!"

"Y'all, must wanna git struck by lightning?" Bert asked.

Jean and I both shook our heads, "no."

"Well, keep acking up and see what happen." Bert warned us.

I don't know how Bert did it all, but somehow, she managed, and with such dignity and grace. When she didn't have money to go to the laundromat, she washed everything by hand. When the electricity was shut off, she burned a kerosene lamp, and if we didn't have anything to eat, she made a lot out of a little. She could even make toast a delicacy. Whenever we got bumps, bruises or bites, she made it all better with Merthiolate˚. A little TLC and Vicks VapoRub˚ was a cure for everything. To say she knew how to improvise was an understatement.

A year later, Howard was released from prison on good behavior. I'd hoped that maybe now Bert would get the break she needed. But what should have been a joyous time for Howard's return home was in fact the beginning of an endless nightmare.

Howard didn't have a job and stayed gone most of the day. When he did come home, it was clear he'd been drinking. They argued constantly about bills, money and food. And on top of that, Fluffy was struck by a car and killed. The following month, we had to pack up and move again.

The house on Myrtle Street may have been just what we needed. It only had two rooms and a kitchen just like the previous house, but smaller. We still had to get our water from the pump, but we finally had an indoor toilet and sink. Bert made the front room their bedroom/living room. The other room was in the back of the house next to the bathroom and the kitchen.

Shawn's bed was on the left side of the wall. Jean and I had the bed next to the window that looked out into the backyard. The dinner table barely fit into the kitchen and could only comfortably seat two people at a time. But like always, Bert made it work. There was a fig tree in the front yard and a pecan tree in the back. But the most exciting thing for me was Washington Street Elementary School was right down the street. The neighborhood was a perfect combination of families and children of all ages, and they welcomed us with open arms.

Our house was snuggled between Mr. and Mrs. Poole (our landlord) and a little girl and her two brothers who lived with their aunt. Mrs. Rice, a widow, lived across the street with her children. A fence surrounded her beautiful brick home and beauty shop. Next to Mrs. Rice lived the Sandersons and Salems. Right beside the Salem's was Nathan Temple Church: Fire Baptized, Sanctified, and Filled with The Holy Ghost. On Friday nights, I could hear drums and tambourines. People were shouting, "Thank you, Jesus!" "Thank Ya Lord!" "Glory!" "Hallelujah!" Bert and Howard never went to church but encouraged us to go. A few months later Jean attended and really enjoyed it. All the members embraced her and took her under their wings.

It was the Saturday before school and Bert took us to B.C. Moore and Sons to do our back-to-school shopping.

"These looks like they'll fit you, Jean," Bert said.

"I can't wear pants anymore," Jean explained.

"Who said you couldn't wear pants?" Bert asked.

"The church. I'm saved now and girls can't wear pants." Jean responded.

Even though Bert didn't go to church she respected it and didn't question Jean about it anymore. We got an outfit for every day of the week, socks, underwear, hair ribbons and bows. I asked Jean what she had to do to get saved because I wanted to be saved too. She invited me to church on Sunday and said they would tell me what I needed to do.

Bert tied two quarters in a handkerchief for me to put in the collection plate. Everyone greeted us with hugs and smiles when we walked in. Jean introduced me to the pastor and told her I wanted to get saved. Pastor Herd was a tall attractive lady with a beautiful smile and a raspy voice. Jean and I sat on the front row. The choir sang a couple of hymns, and the collection was taken. Pastor Herd preached about sinning and going to heaven. After her sermon, she called people who wanted to get saved and join the church to head to the alter. Jean nudged me, "go ahead."

"Anh! Anh!" I said to Jean. Pastor Herd was looking straight at me and motioning for me to come up.

I nervously walked over to her, "This Sister Jean's little sister, and she wants to give her life to Christ."

"Amen," the congregation said.

Pastor Herd asked me, "Do you believe Jesus Christ is the son of God and died on the cross for your sins and whoever believed in him shall have everlasting life?" I nodded yes even though I didn't know I had any sins.

One of the first things I learned was the Ten Commandments and Psalm 23. A big emphasis was also placed on girls and women not wearing pants, piercings or makeup. We also weren't allowed to listen to the devil's music, only gospel. Every member was addressed as sister or brother followed by their name. If they were an elder, they were called Ma or Pa followed by their last name. We were at church at least four to five days out of the week. During revival, it was every night. One thing for sure, it was never a dull moment. Whenever Pastor Herd preached, we could always count on someone getting the Holy Ghost. Especially once the drummer and the keyboard player chimed in. Some turned cartwheels, somersaults, or just literally passed out. Others screamed, cried and spoke in tongues. I wished I knew what made them do that or what they were saying.

The next Sunday Jean jumped up and started shouting. "What made you shout?" I asked.

Jean responded, "The Holy Spirit!"

"Will it make me shout too?" I asked.

She said, "next time just follow me." Jean got up and started shouting and I started shouting too. One night during revival we watched a movie called, *The Burning Hell.* It showed what happened when someone died and went to hell. It was an eternal life of burning. If the intention was to scare the hell out of me, it worked. I swore that day I would obey the Ten Commandments and never sin. I memorized Psalm 23 and *The Lord's Prayer,* as my protection.

On the first day of school, I walked in the classroom and saw Mrs. Matt.

I was terrified. I'd heard she was a mean teacher. She was of medium build with dark skin, well-groomed and wore a short black wig. Tiny moles scattered her rectangular-shaped face. But after being in her class for a few weeks, I realized it wasn't so much that she was mean. She was very serious and no-nonsense. She made her rules very clear: no excuses for late homework, sit up straight and pay attention, and no talking during class. Whenever we took a test, she'd sit at her desk watching our every move through her square-shaped eyeglasses supported by the pearl chain around her neck.

As soon as I got home from school. Bert asked how my day was and what I'd learned. "Take your school clothes off and put on your play clothes. When you finish doing your homework and eat dinner, you can go outside and play." Howard wasn't home as usual. By the time Bert got us ready for bed he was coming in.

"What you cooked?" Howard asked Bert.

"Turkey necks and rice, a can of green beans and canned biscuits," Bert responded.

"Go fix me a plate." Howard was in one of his moods again.

"You can go in there and fix you a plate, I already cooked it." Bert was in one of her moods too.

"Oh, you too good to fix me a plate?" Howard narrowed his eyes. "Then Fuck it!"

"You be alright til you get dat liquor in you. You shoulda stayed where you was." Bert told Howard.

"What you say? Say one mo Goddamn word!" Howard changed his posture.

I was praying Bert would be quiet. I could feel the tension building. but she kept on talking. There was about thirty seconds of silence and then I heard a loud thud followed by a haunting yelp. We jumped out of bed and ran in the room to find Bert wincing in pain, holding her jaw as Howard hovered over her, "Now say another Goddamn word!" I ran over to Howard and started pounding him in his back with my tiny fists with as much force as I could. "Git somewhere and sit down, Jo!" Howard warned me.

"Leave my mommy alone!" I yelled at him. Jean and Shawn were crying hysterically. Howard left the house and Bert told us to go back to bed. The next morning, I got up for school, I almost didn't recognize her. Her jaw was swollen the size of a grapefruit and she had a busted lip. Howard wasn't there but I was afraid to go to school and leave her alone, not knowing if he would come back and beat her again. She assured me she was going to be okay.

We had finished doing our classwork early and Mrs. Matt told us we could share a story with the class. Some told stories of how they went fishing, learned how to ride a bike, or went to eat at a nice restaurant. When it was my turn all I could think about was Bert, so I said, "My daddy beat my mommy up last night and gave her a fat jaw and a busted lip."

The entire class erupted with laughter.

"Joretta! Sit Down!" Mrs. Matt ordered me.

After the bell rang Mrs. Matt made me wait in class until everyone left. "Why did you say that about your daddy? You are one of my best students. I am so disappointed in you. After you do your homework tonight, I want you to write, 'I will never lie on my parents again' one hundred times." I didn't understand why Mrs. Matt assumed I was lying. It's not like she knew my parents; she had never met them. I didn't say it to get a laugh. A part of me thought if Howard knew the teachers knew he was beating Bert, he would be too embarrassed to do it again.

Not only did he beat Bert again, but it became the order of the day. There were nights I was prepared for it if an argument started first. Then there were those nights when I was jolted out of my sleep at 3 a.m. to the sounds of glass shattering and violent screams.

"Lawd Jesus! Help Me!" Bert would alternate between screams and soft utterances.

"I'll break yo Fuckin Neck! You Black Bitch!" Howard would yell at Bert.

"I hope Mrs. Poole and dem hear you and call the police." Bert would reply.

"Let 'em call the law and tell em to call the undertaker too!" Howard was almost daring Bert.

There were times when he beat her so badly and for so long that it woke up the neighbors, and they would call the police. Depending on which police came determined whether he went to jail or not. And he very seldom went the first time they came out. The white male police officers would give him a warning. The Black female officer would tell him to take a walk and cool down. Sometimes it worked and sometimes it didn't. The only time he went to jail is if the white officers had to come back twice in one night, and the only reason why they took him in is because he disturbed *their* peace.

I noticed Bert was drinking excessive amounts of alcohol, wasn't cooking as much and her appearance started to decline. She had also become hostile and angry. No matter how bad things were at home, I made sure to never mention it again at school. Going to school became my refuge. I already had an affinity for reading, Bert started me on the *Dick and Jane* series when I was four. Plus, I saw her reading something every day, either the newspaper or *Our Daily Bread Devotional.* I soared through third grade with Es in every subject except for math. It was not my favorite, yet I was happy to get an S. I used to get excited about going home and showing Bert my report card, but now I dreaded it because I didn't know what I was going to walk into. By the end of school, what I'd eaten for lunch was long gone and my stomach was growling. I'd visualized going home and the aroma of Bert's fried chicken, rice and gravy and canned biscuits meeting me at the door. Instead, I walked in to find Bert and Howard not there at all.

I knew something wasn't right. Howard wasn't working a steady job, he was doing what Bert called, "piece work," a little something here and there. Bert didn't work at all, outside of cleaning the juke joint that one time, I'd never known her to work. But how were they paying the bills? One day Pa Poole came to the door and gave me a note to give them that read, *I ain't got no rent in two months, when will you be able to pay?*

I didn't know my daddy was illiterate until one day he and Bert were arguing, and she made fun of him, "At least I know how to read and write. Yo stupid ass don't even know how to sign your own name, have to put an X for your signature."

"That's alright, at least I can count Goddammit. I bet you can't nobody fool me outta my money." Howard retorted.

"What money? You ain't got no damn money. All you do is let everybody make a fool out you and have you running errands. You ain't paying no bills, we bout to get put out and if it wasn't for me getting that Lil welfare check and food stamps, we wouldn't have lights or anything to eat."

As quickly as they were hurling obscenities at each other, the conversation changed to them laughing and talking. They apparently worked something out with the landlord because we didn't have to move. And for a while, things seemed as though they were improving. Bert took us grocery shopping and let us get whatever we wanted. We filled the buggy with Oreo cookies, Frosted Flakes', Nestlé˙ Quik chocolate milk and Tang˙. All the neighborhood children played together. Missy Sanderson and I became very good friends. The middle of the street was our playground. We played dodgeball, *Simon Says* and *Red Light, Green Light*. When the truck came through to spray for mosquitoes, everyone yelled, "There go the mosquito truck!" And we'd all run behind it playing in the cloud of chemical smoke the truck released to kill the mosquitoes.

It was a Saturday afternoon a few weeks before Christmas when several military trucks pulled right in front of our house. Bert ran to the door, "That's a convoy. I wonder if something happened to Smoky." Several men got out dressed in Army fatigues and went to the back of the truck and started pulling out large black trash bags. They gave Bert the bags and told her Smoky had sent them to us. She opened the bags and there were toys and clothes for all of us. We were so excited and had no idea. Smoky couldn't be with us for Christmas, but he made sure we had a good one.

By the time I started fourth grade, things really started to get bad between Bert and Howard. They were getting drunk on a regular basis, and he was beating her just as regularly.

I thought just maybe my disheveled appearance would raise some concern and the teachers would at least inquire, but no one asked if I was okay. How could they not notice that my hair wasn't combed, the clothes I wore were wrinkled, and sometimes too big or too small? What I did notice was that some of my classmates started to make fun of me or treated me as if I were invisible. It was at that moment that I felt I was different from everybody else. It hadn't occurred to me that my parents didn't have a car, a job, or a decent place to live, and was receiving food stamps because we were needy.

There were girls who came to school dressed in pretty, clean clothes and their hair in two big ponytails, a perfect part down the middle and big bangs. I was ashamed and embarrassed. I dreaded going to school. They could make fun of how I looked, but what a lot of them didn't know was how smart I was, especially in reading and spelling. When it was my turn to read aloud, I could hear them snickering. After I read three pages in less than five minutes, there wasn't a sound. I knew I had to show them not to judge me by how I looked. I immersed myself into learning. It was all I could to deflect the negative attention.

Going home was just as dreadful as going to school. Bert and Howard weren't there most of the time. We were lucky if we got a decent meal. The constant beatings and violence caused Jean to have seizures, and because she started having them at school, they contacted a social worker who recommended Jean be removed from the home. Fortunately for her, Jean was able to go live with Howard's distant cousin, Mrs. Pepple (Sister Pepple) an elderly lady with children of her own. Jean had to attend a different school, but I still got a chance to see her at church because Sister Pepple was a member. For whatever reason, Shawn and I were allowed to remain in the home. Even if I could've left, I wouldn't have because if I did, there wouldn't be anybody there to protect Bert.

We were down to the heels of the loaf of bread and nothing to put between it or on it. I was looking forward to the food stamps coming so Bert could go grocery shopping. Instead, she gave me a book of stamps along with a note to take to the liquor store that read, "I need two pints of Log Cabin' and a fifth of Grande Canadian." I gave the man the note and the food stamps, and with a look of dishonesty and deceit he handed me the whiskey in a large brown paper bag. Bert rewarded me with two dollars in food stamps. I went to the corner store and got a loaf of bread, bologna and some strawberry cookies. I became Bert's liquor store runner to the point I looked forward to it. I had no choice if I wanted to eat because meals were almost non-existent. I was making trips sometimes three to four days a week until the food stamps were gone. Some days I would come home from school and there would be men and women in the house I'd never seen before sitting around drinking, smoking, talking and listening to music.

"This my yelling baby, Jo" Bert said as she introduced me.

"Howard, she looks just you." One of the guests remarked.

"Yeah, but she looks like my mama too, that's Lil Eunetha there." Howard responded.

"You gettin good marks in school?" asked one man.

"Yes sir," I replied.

Bert interjected, "Yeah, she real smart now."

How would she know? She hasn't looked at my homework in weeks. Nor did she know that I was chosen to play the role of Dorothy in the *Wizard of Oz*. And not only did I memorize my lines, but everyone else's lines too. He reached in his pocket and pulled out a dollar bill. "Here, go to the sto' and buy you some candy."

I thanked him and went in the kitchen. For the first time in weeks, there was food on the stove.

If this is what it took to get a meal maybe, they should have company over more often. I had outgrown most of my clothes and had rotated the one pair of pants that still fit with as many tops as I could. I made a concerted effort to be the first one in class to avoid being stared at. It was ten minutes past eight when I woke up. Bert and Howard had overslept. I had nothing to wear and the thought of walking into class late terrified me. I looked through Bert's dresser drawer and got a pair of brown pants and a long-sleeved, powdered blue blouse. The times that I sat and watched Bert take in Howard's pants by hand came in handy. I turned the pants inside out and went down each side with big seams and made about a four-inch hem. I ironed them all around to make it stay in place, took the belt from Bert's housecoat, tied it around the blouse, rolled up the sleeves and left for school.

On my way to class, I was trying to think of the perfect time to walk in without everyone noticing my baggy clothes. Maybe I could catch them during pencil sharpening or maybe someone would be at the board solving a math problem. But when I got there, Mrs. Peterson was at her desk, and everyone was in their seats looking right at her. I thought to myself, *there's no way I'm going in there*. They will laugh me right back out the door. It wouldn't be as bad if my desk was in front of the class, but it was all the way in the back.

I psyched myself up to it and now I was even talking to myself. "Okay Joretta, you can do this, just open the door, hold your head up high and walk straight to your desk." I opened the door slowly and immediately realized it was not going to be good for me. I could see a couple of classmates holding their hand over their mouths to keep from laughing and others looked embarrassed for me.

Out of nowhere, I said, "Oh, I thought it was rag day," and then I broke out in a song and dance. The class cheered me on and forgot all about what I was wearing. Every day after that they requested a show before class, but no song or dance could mask what lied ahead.

Bert and Howard managed to find every bootlegger and juke joint in town. They spent the entire day at those places getting drunk, come home, sleep it off and go back again. I learned quickly where every one of their hangouts were in case, I needed to find them. I became self-sufficient very fast. I washed my clothes by hand and if I had to dry them in a hurry, I placed them in front of the fan. I learned how to cut wood and make a fire and pump enough water to bring in the house for the night. That night when I prayed, I asked God why he gave me these parents and if I did something wrong to cause them to behave the way they did. Whenever I went to church, the message was always about love, faith and forgiveness. As much as I loved my parents. I became angry and bitter at the choices they were making. How hard could it be to stop drinking and become responsible adults?

"I'll blow yo mutha fuckin brains out!" I heard Howard's voice become scary again.

"Go head, do it!" I ran in the room and Howard had the gun pointed at Bert. I jumped in front of the gun.

"Shoot Me! Shoot Me!" I cried!

"I'm sorry baby girl. Imma go to bed and I ain't gon say nuthin else tonight." Howard had calmed down.

"Go on back and git in da bed." Howard instructed me. He looked really sorry, but I believed he was more ashamed than anything. I prayed to God that night to not let my daddy beat my mommy anymore.

After the chorus finished singing, I walked over to the piano and sat beside Mrs. Douglas to watch her play as I would do from time to time. The piano was my favorite instrument and I always wanted to learn how to play. I knew I never would because Bert and Howard didn't have the money to pay for lessons, nor did they care. The only reason I was in chorus was because it didn't cost anything. "When are you going to stop holding back from letting that beautiful voice of yours come out? You do know you have a beautiful voice, don't you? Do you want to sing?" Mrs. Douglas asked me.

I shrugged my shoulders and sung along to Mrs. Douglas playing "Edelweiss," one of my favorite tunes. Mrs. Douglas words stuck with me. Whether or not she thought I could sing, it was the way she looked at me when she said it. A look that said to believe in myself no matter what I choose to do.

I loved music and there wasn't a Saturday that went by (unless the lights were turned off) that I didn't watch *Soul Train*. When Bert wasn't home, I dressed up in her clothes, wig, big earbobs and red lipstick. Holding the brush as my microphone, I stood in front of the mirror pretending to be Diana Ross, Lola Falana or Barbara Streisand. I didn't give much thought as to what I wanted to be when I grew up. I suspected my love of reading would lead me to pursue a library science degree. That was soon forgotten when Bert got mad, cursed me out, and told me how stupid and dumb I was, and that I would never amount to anything. Those words stuck with me too, and sometimes they drowned out the words that told me I could be whatever I wanted to be.

Maybe Bert was right. Aside from being a good reader, what else was I good at? Apparently, she had no idea of how I struggled to stay awake in class after being up all night trying to save her life. Or not being able to concentrate due to near starvation and the only thing I can think about is waiting to go to lunch. Or being in pain because of poor dental hygiene to the point where most of my teeth were decayed, I was ashamed to speak in class for fear they would smell my bad breath. As much as I tried to go unnoticed, Mrs. Peterson noticed my good behavior and called on me to erase the board, go outside and beat the eraser, and monitor the classroom when she stepped out. Now I had to deal with some of my classmates disliking me because they thought she was showing favoritism.

Every day after school, a group of us walked home together. After the other children split off and went in other directions, I was the only one walking home by myself. Right before I got to the catholic school, I heard someone yell, "Hey wait up!" I looked back and saw it was a girl whom I'd never seen before. She was tall and looked too big to be in elementary school. I stopped and as she got closer, I saw she had a mean look on her face. I wanted to run but I didn't want her to know I was afraid. She walked up to me and said, "You think you smart, don't you?" And pushed me to the ground. My books flew out of my hand. She looked at me and laughed that sounded so wicked it didn't belong to a girl her age. I gathered my books, brushed the dirt off my clothes and ran home as fast as I could. I didn't even bother saying anything to Bert or Howard because they weren't going to do anything about it. All I kept seeing that night was the girl's face. Her huge eyes, big, chapped lips and yellow teeth that were all separated. Her uncombed hair was about the length of my pinky. And what little she managed to gather in a pigtail was supported by a red rubber band in the center of her head. She was very unattractive, and her unkindness made her even more so. I prayed that would be the last time I would see her.

I stood in line anxiously waiting to get into the fair. I'd heard some of my classmates talk about how they went every year and how much fun they had. Bert and Howard gave me and Shawn money to go and they allowed us to go by ourselves. As soon as I got inside, I went straight to the booth to see the fattest lady in the world. She was a Black woman sitting on a chair, her face expressionless. A menu was posted on the outside of the booth that listed her daily food intake which consisted of several dozens of eggs and chickens. A song called, "Big Fat Mama" played over and over. There was also the shortest man and the tallest woman in the world. As I looked around at all the people who were part of the fair, I became more interested in where they were from, their families, and how they got a job working there. I thought it must be exciting to travel all over the country and getting paid to have fun. I rode the Ferris wheel, got some cotton candy and a candy apple, then it was time to go home. I had so much fun, I forgot all about the mean girl who pushed me down.

Dear Santa, all I want for Christmas is a green bike and a pair of penny loafers. I have been getting good grades except for math, but I am trying really hard. I wanted the bike because my friend had one, even though I didn't know how to ride. Several of my classmates had new penny loafers and I couldn't wait to get a pair so I could put a shiny penny in each one. I got up at seven o'clock Christmas morning, ran in the room and there wasn't a bike or a pair of shoes in sight. I knew there had to be a mistake. Bert and Howard were passed out. "Bert! Bert! Wake up! Where's my bike?"

She looked at me with a confused look on her face then looked over at Howard. "Howard, where's Jo's bike?"

"Go back to bed. I'll find out what happened." Howard mumbled.

"You were supposed to go down to Coot's house and git the toys before you got drunk and fell asleep." They accused each other of being at fault. About an hour later Howard came back with my bike and penny loafers. When I questioned them about why Santa didn't bring it, they gave me some convoluted story about how he was so busy he left it at the wrong house. I knew before then Santa wasn't real, but I wanted him to be. I wanted to believe he could very well exist just like God whom I had never seen but was told was real and all I had to do is believe. It wasn't so much about believing in Santa. It was about believing that someone cared enough about me. It took months to learn how to ride my bike. Missy's brother had me practice every day. And I ran into the neighbor's fence so many times I put a dent in it, but I eventually got the hang of it.

Shawn and I went to the liquor house looking for Bert and Howard. The man who owned the house told me they weren't there, but I could come in and wait until they got back. He gave me and Shawn a bag of chips and a soda while he and other adults played cards, drank liquor, and listened to music. Hours went by and Bert and Howard never came. As the other adults started to leave, Mr. Shag offered to take me and Shawn to the beach. He said maybe Bert and Howard would be there by the time we got back. He told us he would buy us some clothes, food and toys. I didn't know anything about him other than seeing him when I went to his house looking for my parents. Mr. Shag was a heavyset man, about 5'7, light-skinned with a low haircut. Every time I saw him, he was dressed nicely and wore nice watches. There was one thing about him that made me a little afraid. He had a sinister smile and a glass eye which gave him a monstrous look. He told me to get in the front seat and Shawn in the back.

Once we were outside of the city limits Mr. Shag stopped at a country store to get gas. He got back in the car and reached under his seat and pulled out a gun and placed it by his right side and kept his right hand on the gun while driving. I was too afraid to say anything and when I looked in the back seat at Shawn, I could see he started to cry. I gave him a look that said, "don't cry," and prayed Mr. Shag wouldn't hurt us. He started driving faster and erratically. He was talking but his speech was incoherent. We were on a long country road with nothing but cornfields on both sides. There weren't any cars coming in any direction. Mr. Shag looked over at me, smiled, and said, "Y'all ain't going to no damn beach today."

At that point, Shawn and I started screaming and crying, "Mr. Shag! Please let us out the car! Please!!"

He drove even faster, doing at least 100 miles per hour. Then out of nowhere, he lost control of the car and it veered off the road to the right. He managed to get back on the road and then swerved again. He lost control of the car and was headed towards a tree. Somehow the car ran over something before hitting the tree. The impact knocked him unconscious, causing his head to lay on the horn. The car started smoking. Shawn and I wasn't hurt. Minutes later, the police came. We told the police what happened, and they arrested Mr. Shag and took us to the police station until a social worker picked us up. She told us that Howard was in jail and Bert was in the hospital. And due to the severity of her injuries along with having an asthma attack, she was going to be there for a while.

The social worker drove up to a big white wooden house with chipped paint. Grandma Neat was sitting on the porch in an old wooden rocking chair. A big vegetable garden was adjacent from the house and a huge oak tree stood to the right of the house, concealing a window. I saw several of my cousins standing around. I noticed they weren't as cheerful as most children, instead they all had a look of gloom. "Y'all chillun shole done got big since the last time I seent y'all." Grandma Neat grabbed me and Shawn by the hand. "Y'all come say hi to yo cousin Joretta and Shawn.

My cousins whispered, "Hi." We entered the kitchen, and she told us to have a seat at the table while she talked to the social worker. Grandma Neat was granted temporary custody.

I had only been to Grandma Neat's house when I was very little and my memories of her were very vague. I thought about what it would be like if I stayed with her. She was already taking care of Wade and my cousins whom I could go to school and play with. I didn't know much about her other than the stories Bert told me. She said people came from all over the country to see Grandma Neat about casting spells on people and have spells removed. Bert said she was mean, and a lot of people feared her— including the police. The two weeks I was there was confirmation that something about her was amiss.

Grandma Neat's house had a strange feel to it. The kitchen looked more like a lab; it was dark and dreary with concrete floors and a metal table.

There were no signs of snacks or food. At our house, we kept our cereal and loaf of bread on top of the refrigerator. We had a cookie jar and containers for rice, flour and sugar. My cousins sat quietly, every now and then they would stare at me and then at each other. I was thirsty and because I was used to going in the refrigerator at home and getting what I wanted (at least when we had food) I walked over to the refrigerator, which was twice the size of ours and noticed a big padlock and chain. The look of terror in my cousins' eyes told me that was prohibited.

Grandma Neat walked around the table with a large black pot and plopped a chunk of grits and a heaping scoop of peanut butter on our plates, serving us like prisoners in a mess hall. It didn't seem to matter to my cousins that the grits were hard and cold. They devoured it as if it were their last meal. I pushed my plate away and told her I couldn't eat the grits because they were cold and asked if I could get something else. Again, I was given the look of terror from my cousins. "We don't throw way no food round here. If you don't eat dem grits, you won't eat nuthin else til in the mornin."

I thought to myself *I'll take my chances because I'm not about to eat no cold grits!* I knew better than to say that out loud. "Here, you can eat these cornflakes. There ain't no mo milk. This the only milk I got." I forced myself to eat the cornflakes with powdered carnation milk wondering if I should have opted for the cold grits. After dinner, Grandma Neat showed me and Shawn where we would be sleeping. The room was also dark with dark and heavy curtains on all the windows. There were four beds and a bookcase containing books about witchcraft and voodoo. Grandma Neat told me and Shawn we were lucky to be alive because if Mr. Shag hadn't wrecked, he was going to rape me and kill both of us. I don't know how she knew that but maybe he was going to do something bad to us.

While she was talking to us, I noticed a black cat sitting on the mantle with its eyes fixated on us. Then I saw a second one on top of the bookcase. And then a third, fourth, and the final count was Nine Black Cats!!! It was as if they had been summoned to come watch us. Grandma Neat left the room and turned off all the lights. All I could see were green eyes all around the room. It felt like being in a horror movie. "Shawn? Are you scared?" I asked him.

"Yeah, but I'm going to sleep. Just close yo eyes and don't look at 'em.

The night will go by fast," he said. The next morning the cats had all disappeared.

When it was safe for me and Shawn to go back home, I never thought I would be so happy to see Bert and Howard. After spending several weeks at Grandma Neat's house tilling the garden, chasing chickens back in their coop, and being isolated, home felt like being released from captivity. Bert and Howard behaved as though they were just as happy to have us back. They had our favorite snacks, we played board games, and Bert made us Jiffy Pop Popcorn˚. I was having so much fun I forgot about what happened with Mr. Shag and Bert and Howard never said anything or questioned us about it.

"I dun know who dat is pulling up in dat car." Bert peeped through the curtains just enough so that she wouldn't be seen. "I hope it ain't dat aggravating ass insurance man cause I ain't got no money for him ta day."

"That look like Linda" she said. That is Linda!"

Bert ran and opened the door. "Oh, My Lord!" I didn't know you was comin!"

"I live in Raleigh, N.C. now. I took the day off and thought I'd surprise you." Linda told Bert as she smiled and hugged Bert. "Hey Jo!" Linda gave me a big hug too.

Bert ushered her in, and Linda sat on the sofa. "How you been doin', Bert?" Linda asked.

Linda reached in her pocketbook and pulled a Virginia Slims cigarette from the sleek green and white pack. Crossed her legs, and with one click of the cigarette lighter, it was glowing with red hot embers. She withdrew the smoke and exhaled it in a straight line. I couldn't help but stare at her and how unintentionally beautiful she was. I observed her every move; the way she tilted her head when she talked. And how she flicked the ashes from the cigarette with her perfectly polished nails. Her hair was long, healthy and shiny. Her clothes and shoes were color-coordinated and looked expensive. She had a delightful laugh and a radiant smile that showcased her straight white teeth.

Linda and Bert talked for a couple of hours, with Linda doing most of the talking and asking questions. I knew she could tell something was wrong with the way she glanced around the room. "Y'all hungry? Wanna go get something to eat from Yogi Bear?" She asked me and Shawn.

Linda's car was immaculate. I was hoping some of my friends from school would see me riding in her beautiful gold Toyota Mark II. Riding in a car was something I rarely got a chance to do, and when I did, it was a taxicab or one of Howard's friends taking us to the store. Linda bought me a boo-boo box and a Pepsi-Cola. On the way back home, she stopped by ABC liquor store and got Bert a pint of her favorite whiskey, Grande Canadian. I wished she hadn't done that. Things were good and I wanted to believe Bert and Howard would stop drinking.

"Alright y'all, Imma get on the road so I can get back to Raleigh before it gets too late." Linda took some money from her wallet and gave it to Bert. "Here's something to help you out." She gave me a folded five-dollar bill. I didn't want her to leave and wished I could go with her. I stood on the porch and waved goodbye until I could no longer see her, but the sweetness of her perfume lingered. If only every day could be like this.

The house was in disarray and reeked of alcohol. There were empty liquor bottles strewn across the floor, and the TV was missing. I knew then what kind of night it was going to be. As hungry as I was, I didn't bother going to look for them. I took the one slice of bread that was left and kept hitting the bottom of the ketchup bottle until what little was left splattered onto the bread. Bert and Howard staggered in the house a little after dark. Howard was holding Bert up with one hand around her waist and her arm around his shoulder. I was glad the sun had gone down so the neighbors wouldn't see them. She flopped down on the sofa like a rag doll.

"I don't know what the hell you takin' bout. That ain't hittin on shit." She wasn't making any sense.

"Hehehe, Bert what you takin bout?" Howard was asking as if she was.

"You alright Baby Girl?" Howard asked me.

"What happened to the TV?" I asked him.

"I had to take it and get it fixed. I'll bring it back next week."

Bert was still talking incoherently, Howard was getting angry, "What the hell did you just say!?" Whenever something bad was going to happen, I always got a funny feeling in the pit of my stomach. I tried to keep him distracted by singing and telling him how good I was doing in school, but he wasn't the least bit interested. I kept talking until I saw them both nodding and then I tiptoed to the room and got in the bed. The squealing sound woke me up. I must have been really tired because I never heard them argue, which was the precursor to the beating.

"I'll fuckin kill you with my bare hands!" Howard was dragging Bert across the floor by her hair. His size 15-foot pounding in her side as she begged him to stop, her voice growing fainter and fainter. Howard didn't let Bert go until he heard the police coming. Bert lay almost lifeless on the floor, her eyes almost swollen shut, patches of hair torn from her scalp. The police officer asked if she could tell him what happened. Through her bloody swollen lips, she managed to say, "He tried to kill me." The officer asked if she wanted to go to the hospital and Bert refused. "We're going to take your husband to jail but he'll probably be out in the morning. Do you have a safe place for you and your children to go in case he comes back to the house?" She told the officer she did.

"Coot! Coot!" Bert banged on the door. Bert had taken me and Shawn to her house before, which was just a couple of blocks from where we lived.

We could hear Ms. Coot's dog, Blackie, barking. "Whoever that is knocking on my door, you gon have to come back in da morning!"

"It's Bert, Coot."

Ms. Coot came to the door half asleep.

"Lawd Have Mercy! What done happen to you?" Ms. Coot asked Bert. "You gon mess around and let that man kill you."

"Ain't no way in da hell I'll let him keep beating me like that." Bert held her head down and didn't say a word.

Ms. Coot was a skinny lady with short, thin curly hair. She strutted around the house in short shorts and miniskirts. She had no problem showing her skinny legs that were no bigger than the Camel cigarettes she chain-smoked. She looked mean, but she was a lot nicer than the scowl on her face. She sold liquor and beer but was a little more discreet than the other bootleggers, and she didn't allow a lot of people at her house. Shawn and I were forced to sit there and listen to their boring conversations while being terrorized by her annoying Chihuahua. He would stand right in front of me and bark incessantly before she'd finally say something. "Blackie! Get back over here and leave her alone." Bert fell asleep with me and Shawn on her lap; all three of us cramped in the recliner.

We left the next morning at the crack of dawn. I could tell Bert was afraid to go in the house. She opened the door slowly, but Howard wasn't there. "Y'all stay on the porch until I clean up this mess." Bert had the house clean in no time. The house was cold, so she turned the oven on and opened the door to heat the kitchen. She fried bologna just the way I liked it: six slits around the perimeter with mustard, mayonnaise on lite bread and a glass of sugar water. It didn't bother me there was no TV to watch, all that mattered was I was with my mommy. I prayed that night Howard wouldn't come back.

During the time Howard was gone, there was some normalcy. With scars, bruises and black eyes, Bert carried on. She made sure we ate, albeit it wasn't much, but she made everything taste so good I didn't care what it was.

Missy and I had become great friends. She always asked me to spend the night. As much as I wanted to, I couldn't, because I felt I had to stay home to protect Bert. Missy and I became inseparable. We played, laughed and danced. We rode our bikes to the store and walked and picked pecans, blackberries and apples, and stole green plums off every tree we could find.

We chewed each other's bubble gum and talked until our eyes got so heavy, we couldn't help but fall asleep. There were so many sleepless nights at home, I looked forward to going to her house to get a good night's sleep.

"Joretta, Joretta" Wake up." Missy was nudging me.

"What's wrong?" I asked.

"I gotta go to the bathroom. Come go to the bathroom with me." Missy explained.

"What are you doing?" I asked.

"I have to do the number two." Missy said.

"You didn't tell me you had to do the number two!" I shot back at Missy. "I'm not going to sit in here while you do that! And I don't want to smell it!"

"I'll light a match and it won't smell." Missy promised.

"Ouch!" Missy was so busy talking she wasn't paying attention to how close the flame was to her fingers. She struck match after match until she was finished. Surprisingly, it didn't smell and from that night on whenever

I spent the night, I went with her to the bathroom.

"Hey, baby girl!" I got the TV fixed." I wasn't expecting to see Howard, but it was good to have the TV back. I missed watching *The Electric Company*, *The Brady Bunch* and *The Partridge Family*. Watching TV gave me a chance to escape from the chaos. One day I watched one of Bert's favorite soap operas and I observed how white people drank liquor. They poured it in fancy glasses from beautiful crystal decanters. They were well-dressed and well-spoken, even when they fought. They made drunk look sophisticated. I thought that if my parents were going to continue to drink, then perhaps they should do it with a little more style and class. Drink expensive liquor out of nice glasses instead of red plastic cups. Dress up and speak intelligently because ignorance was running rampant during their conversations. Every time I heard a big word used on a soap opera I didn't know the meaning of, I looked it up in the dictionary and shared it with Bert. My hope was to show her how to be a classy alcoholic. No matter how much I tried to refine them, they did the exact opposite. I poured a little bit of liquor into a glass and gave it to Bert.

"BITCH! What the Fuck you doin?" Bert yelled at me.

"That's how they drink on the soap opera," I explained to her.

"Give me that Damn bottle!" Bert ordered me.

Bert snatched the pint of Smirnoff™ Vodka out of my hand and took a big swig.

"Go sit yo ass down somewhere and git the fuck outta my face!" Bert wasn't playing with me.

Tears welled up in my eyes as I walked away. It really hurt my feelings when she talked to me like that. I felt responsible for her actions and believed it was my job to fix it. If I could find out the reason for her drinking, maybe I could.

I prayed really hard for God to please help my mommy and daddy. And to help me be a better daughter. I tried my best not to aggravate them or get in their way. No matter how hungry or cold I was, I didn't let them know. When the lights were turned off, I did my homework as quickly as I could by the kerosene lamp before it burned out. In the mornings, I got up in the cold, washed in cold water, and walked to school in the cold. I never again asked about why the TV and other household items were missing. (I found out later were pawned.) With no warning, we were packing up and moving again. I didn't know where or why. It was probably because of their fighting or not paying the rent. Whatever the reason, I was devasted. I didn't want to leave my friend Missy.

The front door of the brick house opened to a long hallway. There were four separate apartments, two on the left and two on the right. Our apartment was the second one on the right, beside the bathroom at the end of the hallway. It was the only bathroom in the building and was shared by all the tenants. The only thing it had was a toilet. We still had to wash up in the foot tub. The rule to using the bathroom was it remained locked and the one and only key hung on a nail by the door. If the key wasn't there that meant it was occupied. Except for times when one of the tenants forgot and took the key with them, and we had to knock on everyone's door to see who had it.

It reminded me a lot of the house we'd just moved from. A living room, one bedroom and a kitchen. Only this time, Bert and Howard would get the bedroom and our beds were in the living room. The kitchen was even smaller, but it had a sink and a wooden stove. The kitchen window looked out into a tiny backyard that had just enough room for me to play hopscotch. The wood stump in the ground would eventually serve its purpose. Other than having to enter through the main door and having to share the bathroom with strangers, it didn't seem too bad.

The walk to school was a little longer until I discovered the railroad track was a shortcut making it adventurous and fun.

Bert started to become sick a lot due to having a severe case of asthma.

As painful as it was to see her sick, it was better than seeing her drunk. And even as difficult as the wheezing made it hard for her to breathe, she found the strength to cook and clean. That was the Mommy I remembered. The one who was loving and caring. This was the first time in a long time I'd seen this side of her. Howard was gone all day like usual. Whether he was working was hard to say because a lot of the times when he came home it was late, and he was drunk, and Bert still handled most of the household duties.

If there was one day I looked forward to going to school, it was picture day. The night before, Bert laid out my plaid dress, knee-high white socks and washed and straightened my hair. I had two big ponytails, a pink foam roller to curl my bang, and my hair tied with a silk scarf. The next morning my hair was nice and shiny, and my bang was tight. I was almost by the catholic school when I saw the mean ugly girl standing by the tree. My heart started racing. I walked as fast as I could, praying she wouldn't bother me. I wrapped my arms tightly around my books and looked straight ahead. *Don't make eye contact with her!* I said to myself. As I started to approach her, she stepped right in front of me. It felt like dozens of bees stinging my face. There was dirt everywhere: my eyes, mouth and ears. But most of all, it was in my hair! She laughed and ran away. I cried the rest of the way to school. *It's okay. We're having Shepard's pie for lunch today and I'm going to ask the lunch lady if I can have two cartons of chocolate milk.* I reminded myself. I brushed as much dirt out of my hair as I could. When it was time for me to take my picture, I faked a stomachache. I had no idea who that girl was or why she picked on me, but I was going to have to figure out what I was going to tell Bert as to why there was dirt in my hair.

I could just tell her the truth, but she might try to find out who the girl is. Or I could say I was playing at school, and someone accidentally threw dirt in my hair.

Neither excuse sounded believable, but if I had to choose one, it was going to be the latter. Luckily, for me Bert wasn't in the house when I got home but I knew she wasn't far away because the door was unlocked, and the TV was on. I took off my school clothes and tied the scarf around my hair just in time before Bert walked in.

"How did your pictures come out?" Bert asked me.

"They were okay. I didn't like the way I smiled, but I can take them over on makeup day." I told her.

"Why you got that scarf on your head?" Bert asked me.

"I'm going outside to play and don't wanna mess my hair up." I couldn't believe how good I was getting with believable excuses, but then again, I could tell by the look on Bert's face she knew I wasn't telling the truth.

"I'm finna go back cross the hall over to Rose and Pee-Wee house and finish watching the stories." Bert informed me. "Knock on the door if you need me."

Mrs. Rose and Mr. Pee-Wee lived in the first apartment on the left. I saw them a couple of times in passing but hadn't officially met them. They seemed like a nice couple, and I was happy that Bert had met some new friends. There was an old lady who lived alone across the hall from them. I only saw her once when we first moved in. Shawn and I were the only children in the building. Linda came to visit us again and took me back to North Carolina to stay with her for the weekend. Her neighbors were from India, and their little girl and I were the same age. It was my first-time meeting someone of a different race and country. We talked about the things we liked and what we wanted to be when we grew up. She invited me over for dinner, but I wasn't prepared for what they served and how they ate. We all sat around on the floor and her mother placed the food in the middle on a cloth. There was lamb, rice and some sort of beans/peas I didn't recognize, I didn't like the smell of the spices, and when I tasted it, I thought I was going to throw up. I didn't want to be rude and spit it out, but I couldn't swallow it either.

"Would you like some water?" Her mother asked me.

I nodded yes. When she and her dad wasn't paying attention, I spit the food in my hand and closed it tightly.

She brought me a glass of room-temperature water. I gulped it down and told her I had to go. When no one was looking, I walked over to the sofa and put the food under the cushion. It was getting dark when Linda said she was taking me back to Hartsville. On the way, we passed Limestone College. The campus was beautiful. *That's where I want to go to college*, I said to myself. I was in the sixth grade and had to start thinking about what I wanted to do after graduating from high school. Seeing the college gave me something to strive for. I found out that it was a great liberal arts college. If I kept my grades up, I could probably get a scholarship and major in Theatre Arts or Literature. I just needed Bert and Howard to stay sober and stable long enough to get me out of high school. They were still spending a lot of time at the neighbor's house, which I thought might be good for Bert. Until one day I got home from school. I walked in and heard a lot of noise coming from Mr. Pee-Wee and Mrs. Rose's house.

"Rose! Let em' go! Let em' go! Rose!" When I passed by their door, I saw Mrs. Rose had her husband's balls in her hands, twisting them as hard as she could as he winced in pain.

I heard people laughing and I recognized Bert and Howard's voices. I didn't get what was so funny about that. I could tell Mr. Pee-Wee was in a lot of pain. Mrs. Rose was a tall lady. She was about 6'1" and had strong facial features. She was very masculine with big hands and feet. Her hair was short, and the sides and back were shaved, with a little spike in the top. Her husband Pee-Wee was about 5'7" with dark skin and a big belly. He had a short haircut and two front teeth missing. His voice was high-pitch and squeaky. Her voice was husky. She wore knee-length shorts and a wife beater. He had on khaki pants and a V-neck t-shirt. It was clear she wore the pants. I waited for Bert to come home so I could tell her about my trip to Linda's house, the girl I met and how I wanted to go to Limestone College.

"I don' t wanna hear that shit!" I don't give a damn where you go!" Bert paused and then said, "You can go to Hell if you want to."

I held back the tears and didn't say anything else. I don't know what made me think she would be interested in hearing what I had to say. For the last couple of years, she stopped caring. I saw her giving up. The few times she seemed to care gave me hope that she had some interest in me. But that day, she made it clear I was a burden. If I couldn't share with her the things that made me happy, I surely couldn't tell her the things that were bad. Like the girl who was bullying me or the man across the hall who showed me his ding-a-ling when he saw me go to the bathroom by myself. She blamed me for everything that was wrong in her life. She talked about how stupid and dumb my daddy was and how she hated she had children from him. She told me I was a Fuck she could've saved.

I wanted to believe that maybe she was just frustrated and didn't mean it, but she said it with such conviction, and the look of evil in her eyes said she meant every word. I took those words to heart and believed that perhaps something was wrong with me. Maybe it was my fault for her life being a mess. I told myself I would do everything I could to not make it any harder than it was and to stay out of her way. I cut wood on the stump and made a fire. I washed my clothes by hand and hung them out to dry. In the winter when my jeans froze on the clothesline, I tried to iron them dry. I did the best I could combing my hair and dressing myself. When the lights and water were turned off, I learned how to improvise.

At the same time all this chaos was going on, something even more troubling was happening. Soldiers were returning home from the Vietnam War, many of them shell shocked. Smoky was one of them. He walked the streets in the summer in 90-degree heat in a maxi fur coat with the sleeves cut out. He covered his face with war paint, holding a dagger and yelling, "I hate Pisces!" Other times, he would climb on the rooftop of the high school and scream obscenities at everyone walking by. When he came by the house, Bert wouldn't let him in because she was afraid. His dad and other people who knew him would try and talk him down and eventually the police were called, and he was taken to the V.A. hospital in Columbia, S.C. He never hurt anyone, but he sure did terrorize a lot of people.

There were other mentally ill people roaming the streets as well. One man with nothing on but his underwear and cowboy boots chased little girls and boys. Another lady talked to herself and chased people. I don't think she had any intentions of causing harm, but she got a kick out of scaring us. Then there was a lady Bert knew who was harmless. She walked the streets all the time talking to herself about Dr. Martin Luther King, Jr. I lived in constant fear of these people. And because I had to walk everywhere, and usually by myself, I was bound to run into one of them.

When Smoky was released from the V.A., he went to live with Linda. He was diagnosed with schizophrenia and manic depression. He managed fine when he took his medication. One day he had an episode and chased Linda and Gail with a dagger. They managed to lock themselves in the bedroom. He punched holes through the door with the dagger screaming he hated Pisces, which happened to be Linda's Zodiac sign. She called the police, and he was taken in again. Smoky came back to Hartsville to live after his release. I felt sorry for him. I knew he wasn't the same person anymore. After a while, we all seemed to adjust to his behavior. When we saw he was having an episode, we stayed out of his way.

Smoky would randomly show up at our house. Sometimes Bert would let him in and sometimes she wouldn't. I saw how angry he would get when he tried talking to her and she would cuss him out and tell him to leave. One day he stood in the middle of the street and yelled, "Bert, you Black Bitch!"

"Smoky git you ass out from in front of my house!" Bert yelled back at him.

"You Black Bitch!" Smoky repeated.

"Keep talking shit, Imma call the police on you." Bert warned.

I knew she was afraid of him. I wondered what would have happened if she had just taken the time to talk to him instead of running him away. Over time, I started to get a little more comfortable with him. When I saw him, he smiled and asked how I was doing. It felt like talking to a stranger instead of my brother. I had no connection to him. We were years apart. I didn't see him much growing up and the last time I saw him I was a little girl. Bert didn't have any interest in talking to him and went back in Mrs. Rose's house. It bothered me to see her treat him like that.

"Who dat out dey talkin to you like dat?" Mrs. Rose asked Bert.

"Chile, that's my son Smoky having one of his fits," Bert explained.

"You know the Army messed him up." Mrs. Rose told Bert.

Bert spent more time at Mrs. Rose's house, more than she did at home. I saw new faces every week. The same music Mrs. Rose played was some of the same music played on *Soul Train*. I started practicing some of the dance moves and told myself that one day I was going to be a *Soul Train* dancer. One of my classmates told me she got her period. "Were you scared?" I asked her.

"No, you just put on a pad," she told me. "You'll probably get yours soon." The thought of that made me sick to my stomach. My classmate's mother taught her what to do and expect when she got her period. Bert never told me anything. Some days I would sit at Mrs. Rose's house with Bert and the women cussed in front of me like I was their age. But nothing like the day a younger lady did. I'd never seen her before. She was petite and very attractive with short hair and smooth brown skin. She wore a sunflower print tube top and khaki shorts.

She was so bow-legged; her legs were so far apart and went so far back like they were going to break. I'd heard some of the men say this was special about women. "I know I got some good pussy" she said. All the other women laughed. Except for one older lady who seemed offended. "Hell, you ain't the only one who got a good pussy." Without any regard or respect for my presence, the ladies talked openly about their private parts and things they did to men and men did to them that I shouldn't be hearing and didn't want to hear. I didn't know anything about sex except for one time I heard Bert and Howard doing it, and it sounded terrible.

The curiosity of my ten-year-old mind asked (apparently out loud), "What is a good pussy?"

"Hahaha!!! Oh Lord! she cute, ain't she?" The other women thought it was funny. Bert was in a chair drunk and had no clue what was being said. The men at a table close by were playing cards and drinking. The young lady pulled me close to her and whispered in my ear, "You wanna a good pussy? I'll teach you how to get one."

It was a tiny shack in the alley with a toilet, two rooms, and two windows absent of windowpanes.

The roof was caved in. Several of the floor planks were missing, and the few that remained were splintered and worn. What little junk we had for furniture was placed wherever it could fit. Our bed was beside the window, the big orange steel dresser with chipped lead-based paint against the wall, and an old sofa with torn cushions across from our bed. Bert and Howard slept on an old twin-size bed propped up with cinder blocks in the same room where an old wood-burning stove was in the middle of the floor. In the corner, an old rusty refrigerator with a stick propped against the door to keep it closed.

The music could be heard from our front porch. "Up the Street," as it was called, was a row of juke joints. Howard took me with him, and I finally got the chance to see why he and Bert loved going there so much. It was an alcoholic's playground. There were a lot of people I recognized. Howard introduced me to some of his friends. A lady and her husband were behind the bar. "Disco Lady," by Johnnie Taylor was playing. Men and women were sitting in the booths smoking cigarettes, drinking and talking. Some were in the back shooting pool. Howard sat me on a bar stool and went behind the bar and gave me a bag of potato chips and a soda. Men and women were in the middle of the floor dancing. I saw the lady who said she was going to teach me how to get a good pussy. She was rolling and grinding her hips better than the dancers on Soul Train. "Ah Yeah!" men shouted as they held the bulge in their pants. She was smiling and enjoying every minute of it. Laura looked to be in her early twenties, much younger than the other women. Most of them were in their early to mid-forties whose faces stored a collection of scars and bruises delivered by the fists of their husbands and boyfriends.

"Lemme have a Falstaff." Laura smiled. "Hey, cutie!" Laura winked at me and took a sip of her beer. "Come on, baby girl," Howard said. "Imma take you home." Laura waved goodbye. Cars were parked on the sidewalk and crowds of people were outside. At the juke joint next door, some men were shooting dice, others were sitting on the hood of their cars talking to women.

"I just finished cooking some chicken bog. You want me to fix you a plate?" Bert's voice was toneless, and her face was blank. The front and back door was opened so the heat from the wood stove she cooked on could escape, although the heat outside was twice as hot. Howard gobbled up his food. "We going back up the street. We'll be back later," he said to me. Bert remained silent. They rushed back to the juke joint as if they were going to miss out on something.

I had been giving Howard a hard time and blamed him for everything, but the short time I was at the juke joint with him made me see him in a different light. He worked behind the bar serving drinks and people liked him. The owners trusted him with handling the money. All those times he was away from home, he was working.

There were about four or five houses near ours. Across the street was a girl who appeared to be my age. She wasn't allowed to leave her yard, so she stayed in hers, I stayed in mine, and we talked to each other. Most of the time I stayed in the house and danced and sang in front of the mirror; or played with my doll, I named "Baby Girl," the same name Howard called me. She was my favorite doll even though I was getting too old to play with them. I hadn't seen Missy in a while and couldn't wait until the fall. I was going to start junior high and knew I would at least see her then. I'd finally made it out of sixth grade, even though my grades had fallen due to excessive absences.

School was even farther away; it wasn't on the bus route, and the walk would take twenty minutes. Day after day Bert and Howard went up the street from the time they opened until they closed. Every now and then Howard came home to check on me and Shawn and bring us chips and sodas. I noticed things started to shift between his and Bert's behavior. He became more caring and concerned about our well-being. Bert, on the other hand, had become very cold and callous. She cussed me out daily for something as simple as looking at her. Howard brought her home regularly in a drunken stupor and laid her on the bed. Bert was fumbling with the button on her pants. "What the fuck you looking at me for?" she asked me. "Do you have to use the bathroom?" I asked.

"You need me to help you to the bathroom?" I asked again. The vulgar language spewed from her mouth was my cue to leave her alone. I left the room and minutes later I heard grunting. I ran in the room and saw her in the middle of the floor. "Bert! You're not on the toilet!" I yelled at her. Out of all the times I'd seen her drunk. This was the worst. I cleaned her and her mess up and put her in the bed.

Howard worked the bar, but his pay wasn't much because the lights and water were turned off constantly. And as soon as they turned them off, Howard would turn them back on. He got away with it for a while until the company found out and threatened to lock him up. His illiteracy hindered him from being able to get a good-paying job, so he had to settle for menial and degrading work. He swept floors at grocery stores and took out trash. Sometimes he was paid with food in lieu of money. And it wasn't good food, it was scraps of chicken, pork and beef.

"Look at all this food Mister Mack give me." Howard smiled as he displayed the clear bags of bones that had been stripped of its meat.

"I don't know what you think I'm supposed to do with them damn bones. Bringing this shit in here late at night like you doing something. You a sorry Mutha Fucka!" I felt bad for Howard. Bert always humiliated him. Howard didn't say anything, but I could tell it angered him and I knew she would pay for it. The next morning her face confirmed he hadn't overlooked her comments.

They continued their routine of going up the street and eventually started gathering at the house. Different men and women came and sat at the table and drank liquor. Laura was one of them. She came in the room and told me to follow her to the bathroom. She sat on the toilet and started urinating intermittently. She told me whenever I used the bathroom to squeeze my muscles and hold my pee for a few seconds and release. She said to practice it every day and I would have a good pussy. "This is our secret, okay?" Our house was free to anyone to come and go as they pleased, even when Bert and Howard weren't there. Laura came with a man and told me to go outside while they take care of some business. About twenty minutes later she came out and showed me a twenty-dollar bill.

Bert became friends with a lady who lived a few houses down from ours. She was single with no children, but her huge collection of porcelain dolls was a clear indication of an obsession with children. She was dark-skinned, tiny eyes, big lips, and a deep raspy voice that may have been from the Pall Mall cigarettes she smoked. We would find ourselves having to run to her house late at night when Howard beat Bert. And when Howard showed up trying to get Bert to come out, Ms. Roth would tell him, "You better git you ass off my porch fore I put sumthin hot in you."

She had her pistol in her hand and was ready to use it if need be. "I ain't trying to cause no trouble, Imma leave." Howard must have known what was on the other side of the door because he walked away quietly.

I didn't mind being at Ms. Roth's house when Bert was there, but there were times Shawn and I stayed there without her. When I asked Bert where she was going, she'd say, "I'm going to see a man about a cow."

"I don't wanna stay here." I told Bert.

"Well. you ain't got no choice." Bert said. "What you crying for?"

"I'm scared." I spoke for both me and Shawn.

"Scared of what?" Bert asked. "What you scared of Roth for?"

"She…She looks like James Brown." I admitted. Ms. Roth thought it was so funny.

"Oh Lord, Girl. Roth, don't pay her no mind." Bert apologized to Ms. Roth and left us with her.

The first day of school was just weeks away and Bert hadn't said anything to me about going back to school shopping or to the beauty shop. I was already apprehensive about all the rumors of how seventh graders were treated. The last thing I needed was being picked on because of my clothes and hair. The first day of school was overwhelming to say the least. Thank goodness my friends were there. I knew it would take some time for me to get acclimated, but I didn't feel like I belonged. I was extremely shy and had become even more withdrawn. Bert's constant humiliation caused me to feel insecure and inadequate. The bright side was, I was one step closer to high school, but it was going to be the longest six years of my life.

Bert and Howard's drinking had spiraled out of control. There was not one day I came home from school and found them home and sober. I was tired of having to walk through crowds of drunk men at the juke joint who pinched my butt as I walked by. It was a disgrace seeing Bert slumped over in one booth and Howard in another. They had no self-respect or shame. They aired their dirty laundry for everyone to see and hear. Bert had a way with words and a tongue that cut deeper than a knife. She knew how to get under Howard's skin with her words; telling him, "YOU CAN SUCK MY PUSSY TIL YOU GET CUM DRUNK!" Those words were a guaranteed beat down.

The day I saw Howard brutally beating Bert in the middle of the street, I knew I had to do something. People were standing around looking as if they were watching a boxing match while Howard punched and kicked Bert mercilessly. I spotted an empty 40 (ounce beer bottle) on the ground. I picked it up and hit Howard on the head. The bottle shattered into tiny little pieces. "God Dammit Jo!"

I'd hope this would be the final straw and Bert would leave. After a couple of days, they were acting as if nothing happened. I felt a warm gush of fluid and I immediately knew what it was. School was the last place I wanted to get my period. I was too scared and shy to ask if I could be excused to go to the bathroom. There were fifteen minutes left in fourth period and the flow was getting heavier. I started squeezing my muscles as tight as I could thinking it would stop the flow, but it didn't work. The bell rang and I waited until everybody left. I was walking down the hall and Loretta caught up with me. "Hey, there's blood in your pants. Did you just get your period? Tie my sweater around your waist and come with me to the bathroom." My pants were soaked with blood. Loretta gave me a Kotex. "You need to go to the office and call your mom so she can come get you."

I didn't know whether to laugh or cry at Loretta's remarks. We didn't have a phone and even if we did, I wouldn't dare let my mom come to my school. I stayed at school in my bloody pants until the end of the day. As soon as I got home, I took my clothes off and started washing the blood out of my pants and underwear, but the pad broke into pieces. Bert didn't teach me anything about my period, so I thought I could wash the pad too. She came home drunk as usual. I told her I got my period and needed some pads. "I don't give a damn! You can bleed to death for all I care!" Bert saw my look of frustration. "I don't give a damn about you getting mad. You can scratch your ass and get glad!" A towel served as a pad that night and the next morning. I saw Loretta and asked if she had another pad I could borrow. The

70

following day she brought me my own box of Kotex.

Sheer luck got me through seventh grade. I was determined to go to school and do well if I wanted to go to college. However, things at home were becoming more intense. For every time Howard beat Bert, I broke a bottle over his head. Bert and Howard's friends were still coming in and out of our house, but there was one man I noticed who was a little too friendly with Bert. She introduced him as the landlord, but he was there more than a landlord should have been. Howard found out later that he and Bert were messing around.

It was at that point I started to look at Bert differently and lose respect for her. Bert and Mr. Billy flaunted their affair around Howard as if he didn't exist. Mr. Billy was a slim man with dark brown skin. He had a short, thin stature, but a tall ego. His darkened beady eyes were barely visible under the straw-brimmed hat.

I never knew who was going to be in our house when I got home, but I didn't expect to see a man on top of Bert. I closed the door and sat on the porch. "You stupid Bitch!" She yelled at me. "I'm trying to make some damn money and you're being nosey. Get the fuck from round me and take your ass up the street where your sorry ass daddy at."

Howard was asleep in the booth. I had never paid much attention to him until then. His toes and feet were severely distorted from the pain and lack of medical care for his gout. All the bottles I'd broken over his head left a permanent scar on his forehead. He hadn't cut his hair or shaved in months and his clothes were getting too small. I didn't know whether to feel sorry for him or happy that he'd reaped what he'd sewn. All I wanted was for them to see how smart I was, and how much potential I had and for them to take better care of me so that one day I could take care of them. *Dear God, please help my mommy and daddy stop drinking so I can finish high school and go to college.* I continued to pray and ask God over and over. The harder I prayed; the harder things got.

Two months after being in the ninth grade, I came home from school and like most days no one was there, only this time it felt different. Things were scattered all over the house. I went up the street and Howard nor Bert was there. I went back home and waited until night started to fall and decided to walk back again.

A man was sitting on the stoop at one of the juke joints. I recognized him from coming to our house several times. I also saw Laura and some of the other younger women flirt with him. He motioned for me to come over to him. All the other juke joints had closed, and everybody was gone. "You looking for Bert and Howard?" I nodded yes. "The police locked Howard up and Bert left with Billy."

I wasn't sure what that meant. Went with him where? Was she coming back? All sorts of questions were running through my mind. Mr. John Jr. invited me inside and gave me a bag of potato chips and a soda. I sat in the booth and started eating my chips and he sat beside me. "Annie Mae" by Natalie Cole was playing. Mr. John Jr. put his arm around me. "You shy, ain't you?"

Most thirteen-year-old girls are, I said to myself. I was too scared to leave and too scared to stay. Mr. John Jr. told me how pretty I was and how he had been watching me for a long time. I didn't say a word. Even if I wanted to, the lump in my throat would've prevented me from speaking. I had no idea what he was going to do to me. There was no way for me to leave because I was on the inside of the booth. And even if could make a run for it, he would catch me before I made it to the door.

His hand made its way to my button-size breasts. My heart was pounding, I was feeling nauseated from his alcohol and tobacco breath on my cheeks. He took me by the hand and led me to a room in the back. He took the gun from his pants, "Mr. John Jr. Please don't kill me! Please!"

He laughed sarcastically and said, "I'm not going to hurt you. That's for my protection." Mr. John Jr. pulled out a wad of money and placed it on the table. I lay stiff, with clenched fists, eyes closed so tightly barely allowing the tears to fall from the agonizing physical and emotional pain. What seemed like hours came to an end when Mr. John Jr. grunted a few times, and I felt a warm liquid between my legs. Mr. John Jr. wasn't bothered by what he'd just done. He put a twenty-dollar bill in my hand and walked me to the door. I could barely walk; the pain was unbearable. Maybe Bert will be home when I get there so I can tell her what happened. I opened the door; the house was dark. Bert wasn't there. I sat in the middle of the floor and cried about what had just happened and what was about to happen. Bert wasn't coming back.

CHAPTER 2

Homeless shelters, child hunger and child suffering have become normalized in the richest nation on earth. It's time to reset our moral compass and redefine how we measure success

- Marian Wright Edelman

- Bleach on Colored Clothes -

My parents never came back. After several days, the house was boarded up. I found out from Mr. John Jr. where Mr. Billy lived. Bert was shocked to see me standing at the door.

"Who told you where I was?" she asked.

"Mr. John Jr. The house is boarded up and I didn't know where to go." Are we staying here now?" I asked.

"I is, but Billy ain't gon want y'all here." Did Bert understand what she was telling me?

"Where are we supposed to go? I need to go to school." Surely, I made sense, and she would let me stay there.

"Go find yo daddy and ask him. And you need to leave before Billy gets home." Bert was serious!

I begged Bert to let me stay, but she never let me and Shawn in and closed the door in my face. "Come on Shawn, let's go." I grabbed my baby brother's hand and off we went. Where? I wasn't sure.

Mr. John Jr. was still sitting on his stoop when I got back up the street. He didn't seem surprised when I told him what happened.

"I'll get a room, but what you gon do about him?" Mr. John Jr. asked pointing at Shawn as if he were my pet.

"He won't be in the way. He doesn't have anywhere to go." I explained to Mr. John Jr.

Shawn proceeded to get in the car with me. "No Shawn, I said. You can't go. You have to stay here." Mr. John Jr. was serious.

"Way you taking my sister! Jo, I wanna go wit you. Please don't leave me!" Shawn was in tears.

"I'll be back. Okay." I tried to assure Shawn.

"Be a big boy. Yo sister going to take care of some business. Okay?" Mr. John Jr. motioned with his hand for Shawn to keep walking, then reached in his pocket and gave Shawn five dollars. I fought back the tears having to leave my eleven-year-old brother behind.

Mr. John Jr. took me to a motel on the outskirts of the city. As we approached the window, he told me to slouch down in the seat and turn my head so the lady at the window couldn't see me. The next morning, I stepped on something as I was getting out of bed. "There's a leg on the floor!" I had never seen a prosthetic leg before. Mr. John Jr. wasn't offended at all. He told me he lost it after being shot. I was so afraid the first time I was with him, I didn't notice his leg was amputated.

He dropped me off in an inconspicuous area and I walked to school from there. I went to the library after school to do my homework and stayed until it closed. I walked back up the street when the juke joints closed so Mr. John Jr. could take me to the motel again.

The lady at the motel saw us come so many times I no longer had to hide my face. Mr. John Jr. and I had an unspoken expectation we'd see each other the same time at his place. I walked up the street and his juke joint were closed, his car was gone, and he was gone. My only choice was to take the thirty-minute walk back to Mr. Billy's house.

"Who Is It?"

"It's Joretta. Bert's daughter." I answered.

Mr. Billy opened the door with a frown on his face and walked away. Bert came to the door. Shawn stood behind me.

"Can we stay here tonight?" I asked her.

She didn't say a word, her facial expression spoke for her, of how afraid she was of him.

"How bout close my damn door!" Mr. Billy yelled to Bert.

Without hesitation, Bert closed the door. I had no idea where we were going. I knew Hardees stayed open twenty-four hours and I had enough change to buy a cup of coffee. I added lots of cream and sugar until it turned a creamy caramel color the way Bert liked hers. My plan was to sit there all night with the cup of coffee to give us a reason to stay inside. Around 3 a.m. the employee said we had to leave.

Out of all the things I learned in school and church, nothing had prepared me for a night on the streets in the middle of winter. I wandered aimlessly through the cold, dark, silent streets hoping someone would see me and Shawn and take us in. I prayed every prayer I knew, but no one came to our rescue. I had no idea which direction to go, but I needed to stay close to Hardee's so I could use the bathroom to wash up before going to school. I sneaked in the utility barn of one of the houses in my old neighborhood. I stayed awake while Shawn slept. When the rooster crowed, I knew it was time to leave. "Shawn, it's time to go. I'll find you when I get out of school." I was so exhausted, I slept through every class. There was no way I was going to be able to function at school with no place to sleep. I went back to Mr. Billy's house again after school expecting to stay, and once again, was turned away.

I was at the library and had finished my homework and was looking on the shelves for something to read. I found a book titled, *How to Stop Worrying and Start Living* by Dale Carnegie. I had never heard of him, but the title piqued my interest. When I started reading it, I couldn't put it down. He shared his personal story and those of others of how to conquer and overcome any misfortune by changing our thoughts. He shared a quote by Dorothy Dix called, "I Stood Yesterday, I Can Stand Today." I read it over and over until I memorized it.

I tried my hardest to make things look as normal as possible and not draw any attention. But as the days went on, it became more difficult. My nights were spent trying to find a safe place to sleep. I had to rely on my instincts to get me through and I had to teach Shawn how to do the same when we couldn't be together. Sometimes I was lucky enough to find an unlocked car for us to sleep in. If not, I walked until I got tired and had no choice but to sneak behind a house or tree fighting to stay awake in case I had to run. And there were many times I had to run: from dogs, weird noises and men. Sometimes I got away and sometimes I didn't.

I had just crossed the railroad track and was going behind an office building where I thought it might be a safe place to sleep. A man grabbed me and dragged me behind the building. I kicked, cried and screamed to the top of my lungs. He covered my mouth with one hand and pulled my pants down with the other. I sunk my teeth into his fingers as hard as I could, but he didn't budge. When it was over, I recognized him as the son of a lady from church.

I stayed behind the building until the next morning and ran across the street to the catholic school to get clothes, walked to Hardee's and washed up, and then went to school. I never mentioned what happened to anyone. I wasn't learning much of anything because I was too focused on where I was going to sleep at night. I knew if something didn't change soon, I wouldn't be able to keep up the façade. Occasionally I would see Mr. John Jr., ride out to a long dirt road and we'd have sex in the back of his station wagon. Some nights he would sit with me afterward telling me how pretty I was and how much he loved me, then drop me off at the corner with a twenty-dollar bill.

Days turned into weeks, then months, and I was still on the street. School became less of a priority. Every day I went to Mr. Billy's house after school hoping to walk through the door, sit at the table, eat a hot meal, take a hot bath, and sleep in a warm bed. And every day I was told no.

I was determined to make Bert be responsible. I had so many dreams about how I was going to go to college and make a lot of money so I could take care of her. Either compassion or my persistence got to her because one day she did let me in. "You can come in and eat, but Billy be home after a while, and I don't want him to catch you here." The house was dark and had an eerie feeling. The living room furniture looked as if no one had ever sat on it. There was a bedroom to the left with a glass door covered with curtains, and a second bedroom in the center of the house off from the kitchen. Bert fixed my food never saying a word pacing back and forth. I devoured the plate of fried chicken, rice and gravy, green beans and Pillsbury biscuits. "Oh Lord! There go Billy. He done got off work early." Billy came in the kitchen and put a six-pack of beer in the refrigerator and went to his room. I saw him give Bert a mean look, but he didn't say anything to me.

"Jo, you need to leave." Bert told me. The same feeling came over me that I got when I knew Howard was going to beat her and I didn't want to leave her there.

"Bert! Come Here!" Billy yelled from the bedroom.

"Jo, you need to leave now!" Bert insisted. That night I was more worried about what was happening to her than I was myself. Like every day after school, I went back the next day, and just as I'd feared, Bert came to the door with black eyes, a busted lip and a swollen jaw. "It's yo fault!" I told you Billy didn't want you here, but you keep branging yo ass here anyway. I know why yo ass keep coming here. You trying to watch John Jr." Everybody talking about you Fucking him." That man is married and got chillun younger than you." She talked to me as if I were a grown woman instead of her teenage daughter, she abandoned at thirteen who was a victim of child molestation and statutory rape.

Time was running out for me to find a place to live if I wanted to continue going to school. There was a battle between school and the streets, and the streets had a strong lead. I was spending most of my nights riding around with Mr. John Jr. and saw another side of him. He was a dangerous man. I watched him shoot heroin in every vein on his body he could find. I witnessed him pistol-whip women and threaten to kill men over a card game. Mr. John Jr. was disliked by many but respected by all. As mean as he was to other people, he never laid a hand on me, offered me drugs, or forced me to do anything I didn't want to do. When we were together, I barely said a word. I just listened and smiled. Now that the word was out about us, he didn't deny it, he flaunted it. I sat by his side at his juke joint while he gambled. He marked his territory by keeping me close to him as much as possible. That was his way of keeping the other predators away. But that didn't stop them from offering me money for sex when he wasn't around. And it didn't stop women from treating me like I was their competition. They were women Mr. John Jr. had recycled like paper.

"You think you something, huh? Ain't nuthin special bout you. John Jr. done had all of us. He'll get tired of yo lil ass after a while." I suppose the lady was trying to make me jealous.

After the juke joints up the street closed, those same people made their way to the late-night pool hall. Leos was famous for their fried chicken sandwich. Mr. John Jr. played against other men for money. He kept one eye on me and one on the cue ball. "Go get you something to eat and play the jukebox. You can keep the change."

The lady behind the counter looked at me knowing I was too young to be in there but never told me to leave. It was one of the few places that stayed open until the wee hours of the morning, which reduced the amount of time I had to be on the street. Mr. John Jr. wasn't getting a room anymore, he was shooting up so much heroin, I was scared he was going to overdose and die right in front of me. I knew I had to get away from him.

It had been a while since I had seen Bert. On the way there, a lady and two little girls were walking towards me. As they got closer, I saw the little girls pick up some rocks. "Yeah, you the little bitch I heard was fucking my husband. I ought to beat yo ass!" she said. I ignored her and the rocks being thrown at me by her little girls. "Come on y'all, let's go" she said to her girls. They laughed at me and walked away.

I didn't talk much around Mr. John Jr., but I felt the need to tell him about what happened with his wife. "Oh, she did? You won't have to worry about that anymore. I'll take care of it." I didn't know what he meant by that, but it bothered me knowing I may have caused her harm.

I was introduced to marijuana by some friends I met at Leo's. Once I got used to smoking it without coughing uncontrollably, I got high with men who sold it, so I didn't have to pay for it, but I paid with sex. I didn't mind because having sex was all I wanted to do when I smoked. Some men got a room, the others used their car. I believed all of them really liked and cared about me. I didn't know they were going back telling other men how easy I was.

"You wanna cut a block and get high?" I got in the car and off to the woods we'd go. Even though the attention was negative, it felt good knowing I had something somebody wanted. For so long I had been bullied and mistreated, I just wanted somebody to like me. I had been told I would never amount to anything, I was stupid and ugly, and I believed it. I believed the only thing I had to offer was my body.

One night Laura approached me, "I'm out here tryna make my money but I can't cause you giving it away for free. If you gone do it, you need to make 'em pay for it." I was too afraid to ask for money. When I was with Mr. John Jr. I didn't have to ask; he just gave it to me.

A man old enough to be my grandfather picked me up and drove straight to the woods. On the way back I rehearsed how to ask for the money but hoping I wouldn't have to, and he would just give it to me. Before I got out of the car, I politely asked, "Are you going to give me my twenty dollars?"

"Bitch! I don't pay for no pussy. Now git the fuck outta my car!" he said. "That's why you got a little dick, Mr. Johnson!" I yelled at him and ran away. Lauren who reprimanded me for undermining her business, saw me again and asked if I had done what she told me. I told her what happened with the old man.

"Baby, you always get the money first before you give up anythang." She was familiar with the old man. "Now his old ass is stingy. If you had waited a little longer his ass woulda went to sleep and you coulda picked his pockets. I see now I gotta show you the ropes."

Laura took me under her wings and taught me everything I didn't need to know. She told me she turned as many as seven to eight tricks a day. She told me to keep my feelings out of it, and not to trust anyone, because everyone was out to get me. "Always smile and look a man in his eyes. Men love it when you smile." I watched her interact with men and how she had so much confidence and control. She made it look so easy until the next time I saw her, and she had a black eye. "What happened?"

"Baby, there will come a time when you *will* get yo ass beat. It comes with the territory." I thought about what Laura said, but I didn't want to be a prostitute, I wanted to finish school. I was visiting Bert periodically although nothing had changed except for the cold bologna sandwiches she sneaked me. I got so excited when I saw some apartments and thought I could just move in. The door was unlocked, I went inside and saw it was empty. I left my bag of clothes and books inside and ran to Mr. Billy's house.

"Bert! I found us a two-bedroom apartment upstairs!" I was so excited!

"Jo, what you talking bout? You ain't got no money for no partment'." Bert gave me a sideways glance.

"I don't need any money, it's free. I've already left my stuff there." I told her.

"Chile, you bout as stupid as yo daddy. Go on back where you came from 'fore Billy get home." And the next thing I knew, the door was once again closed in my face.

Well, if she doesn't want to stay there, Shawn and I will. I went back to find the door locked and my things on the ground "Excuse me sir" I said to the maintenance man. "Somebody just went in my apartment and put my things outside, and the door is locked."

"Someone is getting ready to move into that unit and we're getting it ready," he told me.

"No sir! I found it first!" I knew if I explained things right, he'd understand it was a simple misunderstanding.

The man smirked and continued working. Apparently, he thought I was just some kid who was playing around. I honestly thought I could just move in. There were so many things I thought I could do but was completely ignorant of. The time I saw money orders advertised for fifty cents. I asked the clerk for a money order for $100.00. When she asked for $100.50, I was confused because I thought I could get a money order for any amount and only pay fifty cents. And the time two men were discussing a sale on brake shoes, and I told them I wore a size 7 ½ and to get me a pair. They thought I was it funny, but I was serious. I gave more thought to what Laura said but I just didn't have the courage.

My reputation had gotten so bad that one of the teachers called me in the office. "Some of the boys at school are telling me you're very promiscuous and that's not the type of reputation you want to have. Do you want to tell me what's going on?" He was genuinely concerned.

"Yeah, I'll tell you what's going on. I am having a lot of sex and I'm going to FUCK every man in the world, including you Mr. Douglas!"

"Joretta! Get out of my office!" I'd had enough of trying to be a good girl. Clearly, that didn't get me anywhere. I didn't care anymore because nobody else did. I had met some other girls who were in the streets as well, not because they had to. They had a place to stay but their mothers were very lenient. They could get high and drink in front of their mom. I never cared for alcohol considering what it did to my parents. I forced myself to drink just to fit in. They were drinking Mad Dog 20/20, Thunderbird® and White Lightning™ straight from the bottle. Sometimes they got so drunk, they vomited it all back up passed out in the middle of the street.

When they weren't drinking, they were fighting. I didn't like to drink and was afraid to fight. But these girls were tough. I'd seen both get jumped by four girls and take them all down. One time they were fighting, and the other girls were getting the best of my friends and they yelled for me to help. The girl looked at me and said, "You want some of this too!"

"No, I don't have anything to do with it," I replied. My friends got mad at me and called me scary. I wasn't fighting for no reason and getting my hair pulled out and face scratched up. Those girls were vicious. I've seen them cut girls with broken beer bottles and razors. I was the peacemaker and tried to talk my way out of everything. The saying, "Association brings Assimilation" reigns true. Everywhere I went, people were talking about how much we liked to fight. That was not a reputation I wanted either. I was in Junior Reserve Officer Training Corps (JROTC). How and why, I was in that class, I don't know. The teacher asked if I would ride with him downtown to get something he needed. On the way back to school, he stopped by the store. "I'll buy you some candy for riding with me."

"I don't want no Damn candy. I want a beer!" He was speechless.

"Oh, Lord! Let me hurry up and get you back to school." He responded.

There were some mean students in high school, and others who didn't care to learn. I was neither one, but I was thrown into that category. And like most schools, more emphasis was placed on the ones who were excelling. The ones who weren't were left behind. The people in the street at least made me *think* they cared. Teachers saw me as a problem and dismissed my behavior. I was counting down to the day when I could legally drop out. On the days I went to school, I was high, cut most of my classes or attended the wrong class. "Joretta, I didn't know you had me for fifth period. Did you change your schedule? I don't have you for fifth period, this is first period." I had missed four classes and went to a Spanish class I wasn't even taking.

I attended Home Economics long enough to learn how to thread a sewing machine and bake cookies. Some days I wasn't on campus for an hour before a man picked me up. The day I decided to drop out was devastating. There would be no going to prom, pep rallies or walking across the stage to get my diploma. But it was time to put little Joretta aside and get ready for street life.

Any juke joint that allowed me in, I was there—from the time the music started until it stopped. I was in the middle of the dance floor grinding and gyrating like a *Soul Train* dancer. I could hear Laura's voice; "Smile and look them in the eye." Before I knew it, I had a captive audience of men who were mesmerized.

Night after night, men gathered around waiting to see me perform. They would ask, "Are you going to dance tonight?" The attention and notoriety made me feel special.

I had distanced myself from the girls who drank and fought and met some new friends who didn't fight but were notorious for shoplifting. Jena and Jody operated with a team of people and had a system where they all traveled to malls in different cities. They returned with clothes, shoes, jewelry and lingerie. What they didn't sell, they wore. They were "dressed to the nines" every day. Stealing was something I didn't have the nerve to do, but I admired the clothes they wore. A man who obviously weren't too fond of them asked me, "You hanging with them roguish ass girls now? They'll steal the stank out of a shit. You'd better be careful," he said.

I was still getting my clothes from the catholic school and trying to make them look as stylish and fashionable as I could. Every time I saw Jena, she had on a different pair of shoes. I asked her how she got them. "All you got to do is go in the store, put the new ones on, put yours on the rack and walk out." That sounded easy enough I thought. I wanted a pair of penny loafers so bad. I walked in Payless Shoe Source and the manager was the only one in the store. I did exactly what Jena told me to do. As soon as I made it a little way down the road, I heard a man yell, "Hey! Come back here with my shoes!" It was the store manager. He started chasing me. I started running and one of the shoes came off. I looked back and saw he had picked up the shoe, but he was still chasing me and yelling for me to give him the other one. I ran behind a house, and just as I was about to take one more step, a pit bull ran towards me. Luckily, he was tied to a tree and his chain wasn't long enough to reach me, but he was only a few feet away. If I had taken one more step, he would have taken my left arm completely off. I turned around and the manager was standing in the road out of breath, "You wanna give me my other shoe back now?"

I took the shoe off and threw it at him. "Here! Take your damn shoe!"

Jena and Jody knew all the drug dealers. Every weekend the three of us went to a hotel with one (sometimes two), have orgies, and smoked until the room was thicker than fog. When we weren't with the drug dealers, we were at someone's house getting high. It was my first-time meeting A.C., although I knew of him because his parents were long-time members at the church. Jena, Jody and I, along with two other men, were at his house playing cards, drinking and getting high. We were all laughing and having a good time. Shortly after midnight, Jena and Jody said they were getting ready to leave. I started to leave with them and Jena said, "Girl, we're getting ready to go to a room and chill.

I knew that meant I wasn't invited. "Let A.C. walk you home," she said.

"Yeah, I'll walk you home, Joretta," A.C. said. I didn't want A.C. to know I didn't have a home to go to, and I didn't want him to walk with me anywhere. He was strange looking. He was short, wore thick glasses, and he dressed frumpy. Jena could see I was uncomfortable.

"Girl, you gon be alright." She looked at me, winked and smiled slyly. After sitting a few minutes in complete silence, I told him he didn't have to walk me home and I was going to leave. As soon as I opened the door, he slammed it. "You ain't going no damn where!"

"I don't know why you're screaming, because can't nobody hear you!" He put his arm around my neck and dragged me to his bedroom.

"Please! Please! Let me go, I promise I won't say anything." I pleaded.

"Shut up!" He ripped every piece of clothing from my body and threw me on the bed. "I'll be right back, and you better not move!" He returned with ropes and tied my hands and feet to his bedposts. I laid there naked on my back shivering, sprawled over his bed helpless. A.C. walked around the bed degrading me. He called me all kinds of whores, and how everybody was talking about me. I just wanted him to do whatever he was going to do and get it over with.

"Are you going to rape me and kill me?"

He cackled, "You want me to rape you and kill you?" He raped and tortured me until daybreak, he gave me some women's clothing to put on that were too big and allowed me to leave. I didn't say anything to anyone out of fear he would retaliate. Who would believe me anyway?

Despite everything that was happening, I was still going to the library. It was the one place I felt safe and at peace. I read every book I could find on love, healing, self-help and motivation. I read books written by Norman Vincent Peale, Zig Ziglar and Leo Buscaglia who wrote about Love, self-reliance, positive thinking and forgiveness. I felt great while reading them. But when it came time to apply it, it didn't seem to work because things kept getting worse.

I was told that Bert had left Mr. Billy and was staying with a friend. She really wasn't living there; she was just hanging around because she had nowhere else to go. The truth was, the house Mr. Billy lived in belonged to another woman who lived up North and came to Hartsville every once in a blue moon. Whenever she came to visit, Bert had to leave. And when the lady left, Bert went back. There were several women who hung out at Mr. D.J.'s house with him and his girlfriend.

I thought *finally, I have a place to stay* but it was a place for Bert to get drunk. Mr. D. J. said it wasn't enough room in the house for me and Shawn, but we could sleep in his car. Bert was able to stay in the house and sleep in a chair. Sometimes she was there for two to three weeks at a time. If she was there, we could sleep in the car, but when she went back to Mr. Billy's house we weren't allowed to. It didn't take long to see what was going on. Mr. D. J. was having sex with every single one of them, including Bert. Every time he went to the liquor store, he would ask me to ride with him. "I'll buy you some candy," he'd say, trying to entice me.

"No Thank you. I don't wanna go." I said.

"Care yo ass on to the sto wit D.J. and stop sitting round looking in grown folks faces," Bert told me, and she made me go with him. That sick feeling came to my stomach when Mr. D.J. detoured to the woods and told me to get in the back seat. He smothered me with his short, round, humpy-dumpy body, penetrating me, grunting, and sweating profusely. "You don't thank you can sleep in my car for free, do you?" When we returned, no one cared to ask why it took him so long to go to the liquor store that was only five minutes away. After Bert and her friends drank all the liquor Mr. D. J.

bought them, they went looking for more. "Bert, you can't go out there, it's pouring rain." I told her.

"Chile, who you talking to? I don't give a damn bout no rain. It can cloud up and shit for all I care, I'll just dodge the damn turds." She and her friends burst into laughter. I saw a woman who was once soft-spoken and reserved, transform into a vulgar, foul-mouthed, raging alcoholic. My love for her had turned to anger and resentment.

Not many people knew I was homeless. To some, I was just a rebellious, out-of-control teenager. Those who knew, saw it as an opportunity to take advantage knowing there would be no repercussions. Men had a field day with me, passing me around like a collection plate at church. I pretended to enjoy it, but deep down inside, I detested everything about men. Sex became a recreational hobby I strived to have with as many men as possible so they would leave me alone. A breakthrough came when a lady from church who lived alone said I could stay with her. She laid down her rules: no, smoking or drinking, and I had to be in by 6 p.m. I was happy to have the opportunity to be off the streets and in a nice home. For two weeks everything was fine until I came in at ten minutes after six. "Mrs. Holly, why are my things outside?"

"I told you to be in at 6 p.m.!" Mrs. Holly wasn't playing!

"I...I...I was at the library." I tried explaining.

"I don't wanna hear it. Now get your things and leave!" Tears started to well up in my eyes.

"Okay, thank you for letting me stay here." This is what I said to her, what I really wanted to do was yell at her, *that's why you look like Mr. Potato Head!* I wanted to say that to her so badly. There I was, back on the streets. All I wanted was a place to stay so I could go back to school. There were people I hung out with who didn't care about going to school, reading a book or learning anything. Many of them didn't know how to read or couldn't read well. I always tried to read something to keep my mind off what was going on. I needed money but wasn't old enough to work.

I thought I'd give what Laura taught me another try. I went to the catholic school and found a mini dress, a pair of red high heel shoes, and a tube of old red lipstick. I smeared the lipstick on my lips, eyelids and cheeks, and walked up and down sixth street with the shoes slipping off my feet looking for a customer. A man in a brown Electric 225 pulled up beside me. I had seen him a few times before. "Girl! What in the hell that is you got on?"

"I'm a prostitute. You got twenty dollars?" He laughed hysterically, but I was serious.

"Girl, get in the car." P.J. and I rode around and got high. He got me something to eat and before he dropped me off, he gave me twenty dollars. "You ain't no prostitute, you too cute for that." I couldn't believe a man gave me some money without wanting anything in return. I saw P.J. a few times a week, and sometimes weeks would go by without us seeing each other. He was tall, dark, slim, with dark sexy eyes and a beautiful smile. I called him my Black Elvis Presley. I knew where I stood with him. We hooked up, got high, and had sex. I never expected anything more. I appreciated the fact that he was kind.

It had been a while since I had seen Jena and Jody. They invited me to a house party. It was my first time meeting the people there, but they seemed cool. Jena called me to another room where there were men and women sitting at a table. "Come on," Jena motioned for me to join her.

"No, that's okay. I don't want to." I wasn't into it at all.

"Jena, where in the hell did you get this Lil girl from?" The man was clearly upset I didn't want to participate.

"Come, on Joretta. Try it. It's good." Jena tried coaxing me. I didn't want to, but the peer pressure got to me. I pressed down on one nostril and inhaled the white powder through the other. I felt a burning sensation and started sneezing. It was one of the worst feelings I'd ever experienced.

"Jena, you mean to tell me this girl ain't never done blow?" One of the men was pretty angry. I guess I wasted his stash. "Get her the fuck outta here!" I was happy to leave. I didn't like using nasal spray for my sinuses, let alone sniffing something up my nose. That would be my first- and last-time trying cocaine. Jena and Jody were a lot more daring than I was when it came to experimenting with drugs. I had seen what drugs had done to other people and didn't want to end up like them. As bad of an influence as they were on me, I still liked hanging out with them. Perhaps it was their fearlessness, just in the wrong areas. Cocaine wasn't the only thing they were doing. They were into uppers and downers, Quaaludes, Purple Microdot and Christmas Trees.

Taking a pill was easier than snorting something up my nose. Pills allowed me to hallucinate for hours and escape from my reality into a world where I could do and be anything I wanted. But when my high came crashing down, it sent me into a depression like I had never felt before. I was tired of living that lifestyle but didn't know how to get out. I had seen the devastation it caused so many people, and if I didn't soon get out, I was going to be next. The hope of going back to school was slim to none. I had no skills to do anything. Maybe I would meet a nice man, get married and become a housewife. I was still seeing P.J. every chance I could, marrying him was out of the question because he already had a wife and plenty of women on the side who were fighting to be his mistress.

"You want a ride?" David was the boyfriend of a family member I was close to. "Where you going?" he asked.

I asked him to drop me off at Greenlawn cemetery. There was a huge shade tree where people gathered to drink beer and shoot the breeze. We had to pass the elementary school to get there, and David told me to slide down in the seat so no one would see me.

"You know how some people talk. They might see you in the car and think something going on." When he told me to sit up, we were long past the school.

"Where are you taking me?" I asked him.

"Don't act like you don't know what's going on. I heard all about you." David made sure I saw his gun, and I knew he didn't mind using it. He was abusive to his girlfriend and had already shot her several times. After raping me, he drove me back to town.

"You better not tell nobody, or I'll kill you." And he meant every word. Even more traumatic than the rape itself was not being able to tell anyone. Nobody gave a damn about a poor little Black girl with a bad reputation. If I went to the police, I ran the risk of the men not going to jail and I would still be on the street where they could easily find me.

Yet, I still had to smile and speak to them whenever we were in the same setting so nobody would know. These were men who had wives and were well known and liked in the community but were evil enough to hold a gun to a little girl's head while she cried out to God begging him not to rape her, but they did it anyway. And when they were done, they went home and got in bed with their wives like nothing happened. Men who were considered middle-class and lived in better neighborhoods. They came to the hood to buy sex, drugs, and rape underage girls and women they knew they could take advantage of. My only hope was that one day they would reap what they sowed. Somehow, some way I had to get back into school. I talked to Mr. Andrews, and he told me he was teaching night school and convinced me to start.

CHAPTER 3

If you are not willing to learn, no one can help you. If you are determined to learn, no one can stop you.

- Zig Zigler

- Bleach on Colored Clothes -

It felt so good being back in a classroom even though I was behind and had a lot of catching up to do. Mr. Andrews made sure I had everything I needed: books, paper, pencils, etc. "I want you to get your diploma. I'm here to help you. If you come to night school and come on time, you can do it." I thanked him but wondered why a white teacher cared about me getting my diploma. Evidently, he saw something in me no one else did. I kept my word and showed up every time on time.

"Why you standing out here?" Harry asked.

"I'm going to night school and waiting for class to start." I explained.

"You wanna cut a block?" Harry asked me.

"No, class starts in thirty minutes, and I don't want to be late."

"Come on, get in. I'll bring you right back." The few times I had seen Harry, he was always nice to me. I didn't get the funny feeling in my stomach like I did when I got in the car with some of the other men. Harry didn't drive in the direction leading to the woods like other men. He drove around the city as agreed and parked just a few blocks from the school. He passed me the joint. Any other time I would have been delighted to smoke, but I was serious about getting my diploma and I didn't want to let Mr. Andrews down.

"I can't. I have to go to school." I reminded him.

"Relax. why you so uptight?" Harry was beginning to scare me.

"I need to get to school. You can take me back now." I was practically begging him.

"Oh, so now you wanna play hard to get? You know what time it is!" Harry looked angry.

Harry wasn't being aggressive, and he even smiled as he talked to me. I told myself to stay calm and be polite so I could make it back to school. "So that's how you gonna be? Well, if you want to go to school, you can walk." I only had a few minutes to get there. If Harry took me, I would be on time, but if I had to walk, I would be late for sure.

Before I could open the door, Harry grabbed me. "Take your clothes off!" Harry ordered me.

"PLEASE! DON'T!" I begged him.

"Imma ask you one mo damn time. Take your clothes off!" How could I be so stupid to trust him? How could he be so bold as to park so close to the school? He parked there intentionally knowing no one would suspect anything. I could hear cars passing by, unaware I was being raped in the back of the white van. Harry's behavior was just like the other men who had raped me; it didn't faze him at all. When it was over, he tried to carry on a conversation as if we had just made passionate love. "What books dem is you reading?"

I held onto my books tightly ignoring him, wondering what Mr. Andrews was thinking as to why I didn't show up for school.

Harry stopped at a gas station. "You wanna a beer?"

I didn't answer.

"Lemme see what you reading." He snatched the books out of my hand. "You ain't gon need these no mo." The pain of watching him throw my books in the dumpster felt almost as bad as the rape. "You don't need to go to school no mo; school done played out." To make matters worse, he dropped me back off at school, knowing class was over. This time I gave myself permission to cry a little bit harder and longer than I normally did.

90

I owed it to Mr. Andrews to tell him what happened, but why bother? He wouldn't believe me.

Several months after the rape I started having sex with P.J. on a regular basis. When I missed my period, the thought of being pregnant never crossed my mind. When I told P.J. I was pregnant, he asked, "How do you know it's mine?"

As harsh as it was, I suppose it was a valid question considering my track record, but except for Harry raping me, P.J. was the only person I had been with, and I had a period after the rape (thankfully!). From that day forward, P.J. avoided me and never talked to me again.

I told Bert, she told Gail, and she took me to Columbia to live with her. So much time had passed since I had been around her it felt like being with a stranger instead of my big sister. I didn't know what to say to her and she was asking me a lot of questions. "Why weren't you using birth control? Who is the father? Does he know? You know you're going to have to go back to school."

What she should've been asking was: *where was I living and why wasn't I in school?* I knew Gail meant well, and I was appreciative of her help. But I had some feelings of anger and resentment. Gail assisted me with getting prenatal care, and I had access to good food and a beautiful place to stay, but I felt out of place. I had become so accustomed to being mistreated, I didn't know how to accept help. I was so used to being in fight-or-flight mode, I was scared to let anybody get too close to me. "We have to see about getting you back in school." Gail announced one day.

"I'm not going back to school. School has played out." I responded without any emotion.

"What! Where did you get that from?" Gail tried not to lose her temper. "How are you going to take care of your baby without a high school diploma? If you don't go back to school, you at least need to get your G.E.D., go to Job Corps, or do something. Unless you plan on being on welfare the rest of your life." I knew everything Gail was saying to me was true, but I wasn't ready to hear it. I just sat there with my head hanging down. Gail was sincere, but what she didn't realize was the help I needed went far beyond a place to stay and going back to school. I needed serious psychological counseling. I woke up every day thinking it was going to be my last, so planning for a future was more like a dream than reality.

Every day Gail went to work, I was at home sleeping, eating and listening to music. I saw she was getting a little annoyed with my being there and not doing anything. Linda came over and I overheard them talking about me. Linda asked Gail, "How is she doing? Did you talk to her about going back to school?"

"She said she's not going back, and school has played out," Gail explained.

"What kinda shit is that? What is she going to do when the baby is born?" Linda asked.

"I don't know. I tried talking to her, but she doesn't say much." Gail said. I wished I had the guts to go in the room at that moment and tell them that if maybe they had taken me in years ago, I wouldn't be in this predicament.

After I have my baby, I'm going back to Hartsville, get an apartment and get on welfare. I said to myself in response to their conversation about me. I really didn't have a clue as to what I was going to do. I thought that somehow everything would magically work itself out.

"You got a pack a Kool-Aid and some sugar I can borrow?" Terry, Gail's upstairs neighbor asked.

"What flavor you want?" Gail asked him.

"You got Red?" Terry responded.

"I don't know why his ass can't go to the store and buy some damn Kool-Aid and sugar." It was apparent from Gail's remarks this wasn't Terry's first time asking. Terry was a construction worker with medium height, big, beautiful, mesmerizing eyes, thick eyebrows, and a big smile with a gold crown around one tooth. His thick southern drawl along with a speech impediment made it difficult to understand what he was saying at times, but he was down to earth and very friendly. He was a huge fan of Prince. So much so that he competed and won several Prince look-alike competitions.

After work, he invited me upstairs to listen to Prince trying to impress me with singing the words to every song *off-key*. Over time, the attraction grew stronger that would eventually lead to sex. The only thing stopping me was being pregnant. I heard older women say that having sex while pregnant with anyone other than the father would cause the baby to be born illyform (birth defect).

In January I gave birth to a beautiful baby girl. I was excited and afraid at the same time. I had this beautiful little human being who was relying on me for all her needs and had no idea how I was going to provide. I was clueless as to how to care for a baby. I touched her long enough to feed, burp, and change her diaper, and left the rest for Gail. Linda adored her and came over every chance she could. Six weeks later I was upstairs at Terry's apartment listening to Prince's music, smoking lots of weed, and having lots of sex. I was spending more time with Terry than I was with my baby. Gail knew I was headed for trouble and tried to deter me by telling me how easy it was to get pregnant again. I ignored her. When she refused to watch Kee-Kee, I took her upstairs with me.

When Kee-Kee turned five months old, Gail told me she was taking me back to Hartsville. That got my attention. I didn't know it was already decided that I was going to stay with Bert and Mr. Billy. I had no desire to live with them after all I had been through. I played out the scenario over and over in my head how it could possibly work: *I could go back and make the best of it by going back to school while Bert watch Kee-Kee. But can I trust her with my baby after the way she treated me? Or I could stay there until I find a job and get a place of my own.* Both seemed farfetched. I could ask Terry if I could stay with him. After all, we had been seeing each other for a while.

"You alright? Look like you got a lot on yo mind." I nodded yes. "Somethin you wanna tell me." I shook my head, no. I didn't have the courage to ask Terry if my daughter and I could live with him.

"Gail told me you was going back to Hartsville. Is that what you wanted to tell me the other night? I hate to see you go. Do you wanna go back?"

I told him no, then jokingly said, "We can stay with you." I regretted saying it as soon as I saw the look of, I don't think so on his face.

"Nah, you need to finish yo education. But you will always be my Lil friend. I never told you before, but I got a girlfriend. We been together for six years."

He said she lived an hour away and they only saw each other on weekends. The following weekend I was on my way back to Hartsville with my baby.

"You gon need to wash dishes, mop the floor, help me cut wood, and keep dat baby quiet, cuz Billy don't like a whole lotta noise." After laying down the rules and regulations, Bert seldom said two words to me. I sensed her nervousness about my being there and felt like she was watching my every move to make sure I didn't do anything to get her into trouble. I didn't want to be there no more than they wanted me there. Watching her cook Mr. Billy steak and potatoes and having me serve it to him while I ate cold bologna sandwiches sickened me. He always ate in his room, on the bed, propped against pillows with his legs crossed watching TV. I stood at the doorway with the tray expecting him to come get it. "Brang it over here," he commanded. How many times are his boney wrinkled fingers going to *accidentally* squeeze my nipple?

I wanted to work but didn't even know how to apply for a job. Mr. Higgins had several farms and hired me to pick corn and field peas. I was up every morning at five o'clock waiting for him to pick me up. I jumped on the back of his truck with some other people and picked peas from sun-up to sun-down. The pay was five dollars a bushel, which seemed easy until I saw how big a bushel was. I barely picked one the entire day. Working in the fields was drudgery. I came home every day extremely exhausted. Yet I did as Bert and Mr. Billy asked of me. Halfway into August, I started feeling really fatigued. I attributed it to the long days and scorching heat. I was so concentrated on trying to pick a bushel, I didn't remember getting my period for the month of June or July.

August came and went, and still no sign of it. I started to worry. *Please don't let me be pregnant again.* Kee-Kee was just six months old. I couldn't say anything to Bert. When my clothes started getting tighter, it was obvious. When Bert and Mr. Billy came near me; I turned my back to them. I wore oversized clothes to conceal it. "How long you gon keep trying to hide yo stomach." Guilt was written all over my face as Bert began to grill me. "I know you pregnant again. What you gon do with that baby? Billy said you ain't branging another baby in this house." There was nothing I could say. I didn't know what I was going to do.

Mr. Higgins saw I was pregnant. With a big grin, he said, "I knew something had to be wrong wit you, cause every last one of my crops you picked died." My second pregnancy was much harder. I was depressed and scared all the time. The closer it got to February, the more anxious I became. The winter that year was much colder than before. The house was so cold at night I dreaded changing Kee-Kee's diaper for fear she would sustain frostbite from being exposed to the extreme temperatures.

Also, that year, the only hospital in Hartsville was no longer delivering babies, so I had to go to a city thirty minutes away. "Girl! You bout to have that dat baby!" Bert ran to the neighbor's house and called the ambulance. I got to the hospital just in time. It wasn't my intention to give birth naturally, but I didn't have a choice.

"It's a girl!" the doctor said. I was in so much pain, I showed no emotion.

"Here's your baby!" The nurse came in the room holding her wrapped in a pink blanket, but I didn't reach for her. "You don't wanna hold your baby?" the nurse asked me. I said no, in a snappish tone. "Okay, you had a tough labor and I know you're tired. Get some rest and I'll bring her back later." What the nurse didn't know was I had already made the decision to give my baby up for adoption. She returned later with my baby again. "Are you ready to hold your baby now?"

"No, I don't want to because I'm giving her up for adoption," I said to her.

"Oh Lord Have Mercy! You What? Well, if you don't want her, I'll take her." She took off down the hall with my baby. I could hear her talking to the other nurses. "The girl down the hall said she don't want her baby and she's giving her up for adoption." She returned with another nurse. I guess because they were both Black, they assumed they had the authority to criticize me.

"Baby, don't you know Black folk don't give their children away? You need to keep your baby."

"I've already talked to a social worker, and she told me to call her once I delivered," I explained.

"Lord Jesus! Please help this poor child. Why don't you at least take her home and think about it before you do that?"

I gave in and held her and immediately fell in love. I really didn't want to give my baby up for adoption, but I was thinking about what Bert said. The nurses were happy to hear I had changed my mind.

"What are you going to name her?" They all wanted to know.

"Nothing," I responded.

The nurse looked at her and said, "Ashley. She looks like an Ashley."

When I was released from the hospital, I felt I at least owed Terry the opportunity to see her. He made the trip to Hartsville. He seemed to be more concerned about his girlfriend finding out than he did my well-being. I told him I wasn't going to be able to keep her there. He probably thought I was just saying that for sympathy, but I knew Mr. Billy was serious. Terry didn't have a solution and went back to Columbia leaving me to fend for myself.

"Please don't cry. You're going to get us in trouble." Ashley cried constantly. It was a cry that made me cry. I paced the floor rocking her, trying to soothe her, but nothing helped.

I heard Mr. Billy from his bedroom tell Bert, "Go in there and tell that gal to shut dat baby up!"

Her crying agitated me so much I became angry at her. I didn't know why I was having those feelings, but I knew they weren't normal. Postpartum depression wasn't even talked about during that time. I looked at the pillow and looked at Ashley, and knew she wasn't safe with me. The next day, I called the social worker.

"How old is your other little one?" She asked me.

"She's one," I replied.

"We can take her, but I will tell you it's going to be much harder for her to get adopted. Most couples are looking for newborns."

"Well, I guess not." She handed me a stack of papers to sign as she explained the process.

She explained to me once I signed the papers, I was giving up my parental rights and couldn't change my mind. She said it was a closed adoption and I wasn't entitled to know anything about it. I answered yes to all the questions and signed the documents. When she asked if the father was also willing to sign over his rights I told her yes, but that was a lie. Terry didn't know anything about what I was doing. No one did until Bert walked into the living room.

"Jo, who this woman, and what she doing here?"

"Ma'am, I'm a social worker with the Department of Family and Children Services. Your daughter is giving her baby up for adoption."

"What Baby! Jo, I know damn well you ain't fin to give dat baby away!

96

Lady, you need to get yo ass out of this house!" Bert picked Kee-Kee up. "I bet you won't take this one."

"Ma'am, it's your daughter's decision."

Bert was yelling and cussing at the social worker. I continued signing the papers. If I didn't know any better, I would've believed Bert really cared. But it was nothing more than a performance. I held Ashley one last time before handing her over to the social worker. Bert ran out of the house and came back with several of the neighbors. They were all crying and praying, "Please forgive her God!"

"It's just like death—you can't brang her back!" One of the neighbors said. They may as well have stoned me to death. When night came, it made it worse. I felt terrible about what I had done. It really did feel like death. Not knowing where my baby was and the realization of never seeing her again was an indescribable feeling. There was nothing I could do but cry myself to sleep.

"Billy mad at you bout what you did. He said, everybody gon think he the reason you gave dat baby away." Bert was acting like she had a conscience.

"You told me he said I couldn't bring another baby in his house." I shot back.

"Well, you know he wasn't gon put you out," she said. I told myself all Mr. Billy was trying to do was save face.

I didn't want to talk about it anymore. I was already being tormented mentally. People were still coming to the house wanting to see the baby not knowing I had given her up. Jean, Gail and Linda gave me the third degree. Terry made me feel the lowest. "You mean to tell me you're that low down!" Even a dog will fight you if you try to take her puppies. And you can just give your baby away? You're worse than a Dog! I'm going to get her back and you ain't never got to worry about seeing her again!"

I had never seen that side of Terry before. I commended him for stepping up, but it wasn't like I didn't forewarn him. Terry fought tooth and nail to gain custody of Ashley. Having to submit to a paternity test, court costs, and traveling back and forth. The only thing that saved him was the fact that he never consented to the adoption. Now that Terry had Ashley, the mental anguish was a lot less severe. Yet, in the back of my mind, I thought there was still a chance for us to be a family. Terry, on the other hand, didn't give me a second thought and went on with his life.

The word got out around town about what I had done, and the rumor was I gave her up for adoption because she was half-white. After the dust settled, everyone went back to being who they were all along. Bert and Mr. Billy were even more cold-hearted and cruel towards me. They constantly reminded me of how I embarrassed them, as if they were model citizens.

"Take Billy his food." Bert ordered me.

"Why can't he come get it?"

"Who in the hell you talking to like that? You done gave yo baby away, now you talkin shit?" Mr. Billy wasn't going to stop touching me, so I had to avoid being around him alone. Bert kept insisting I take him his food and I kept refusing. "Take Billy his food before it git cold!"

Before I knew it, I blurted out, "Every time I go in there, he feels my breasts!" I quickly realized that was the wrong thing to say.

"What did you say?" Bert's eyes were bulged, she stared at me, her lips trembling. "you're telling a Goddamn Lie! You lying! You Yellow No-Good Whore!"

"I'm not lying!" I wished I hadn't said anything and could take it back. But it was too late. Bert ran in the room and told Mr. Billy what I said. He vehemently denied it, and Bert believed him.

"I let you stay here and you gon lie on me like that?"

"Bert, I'm not lying on him!" I pleaded.

"You is lying! Billy ain't done nuthin but try to be good to you. This my man! And I love him! More than you! More than GOD!" Billy was proud to hear Bert defending him like that. He had a smirk on his face. He knew he had trained her well.

"Don't say nuthin else to her Bert. Let her git her shit so she can git out of my house." They told me I had to leave but Kee-Kee could stay.

It was February, the temperature barely got above twenty degrees. There was nowhere for me to go with a one-year-old baby, so I left her behind. Before I walked out the door, I looked Bert straight in the eye and said, "I will never treat my child the way you treat me."

The same people were still in the streets doing the same thing. I took my chances getting into cars with men. But this time I was vigilant about not being raped. But there were countless times I had to jump out of cars and run through briar patches. No matter what I was doing in the streets, I made it my business to see Kee-Kee every day and she was always happy to see me. To get to Mr. Billy's house I took the shortcut through the cemetery. I would see the same men gathered under the tree drinking beer and listening to music. One of them always tried to talk to me, walking alongside me, telling me how cute I was and how much he liked me. I ignored him and kept walking.

This went on for months and I kept telling him no. I saw him at the club one night. He walked up to me and whispered in my ear, "Can I see you tonight?" Something about the way he said it turned me on. He told me where he lived and said I could come by when I left the club. I was tired and needed a place to sleep so I didn't have to think twice about going. His house was cozy, warm, very neat and clean.

Other than Terry, Tony was the only man I had met who lived alone. I was expecting to take my clothes off, have sex and hopefully spend the night. But Tony was different. "Out of all those months chasing you, I finally got a chance to see you." Tony's words sounded so sincere. "Why are you sitting so far away? Come closer. I'm not going to bite you." He said in a soft, low tone.

Something was happening that never happened before. Tony hadn't even touched me, but I could feel him. He took my hand, placed my finger in his mouth, and caressed it with his tongue before slowly pulling it out, sending a wave of electricity through my entire body. He nibbled gently on the outer part of my ear, sliding his tongue in and out. I flinched from the delicate kisses of his soft full lips on the nape of my neck. My breathing got heavier.

Tony slid his tongue in my mouth, across my teeth, sucking my top and bottom lip. No one had ever kissed me like this before. His hands never left me.

He slowly undressed me and kissed every inch of my body from head to toe, front and back. I looked down and couldn't believe something so big and beautiful was attached to his body. Tony was only 5'8" with small hands and feet. He slid right in and made love to me like nobody's business.

My body quivered and tingled in excitement as liquid oozed out like juice from a succulent South Carolina peach. For the first time, I felt what it was like to be loved.

Beep! Beep! "Oh Shit! That's my ride!" Tony jumped out of bed, threw on his pants and shirt. He ran in the bathroom to wash his face and brush his teeth. I was looking for my clothes to put on so I could leave. "You don't have to leave right now. Go back to sleep. Just make sure to lock the door when you leave. I'll see you later." Tony kissed me on the forehead and left for work.

All I could think about was Tony and how he made love to me, and I didn't want that feeling to ever go away. He was the only man I wanted. I saw it as a blessing from God that I finally had a man who truly loved me for me. The love we had for each other was so strong, I couldn't imagine anything going wrong. If there was one thing I should've learned from past experiences, it was to ask up front, "Are you married? Do you have a girlfriend?" Tony wasn't married but he did have a girlfriend he'd been with for years. They had a unique situation. She still lived at home with her parents who were very strict. So, their time together was limited. As hurtful as it was, I was in too deep to stop seeing him. Plus, I totally ignored the huge picture of them sitting inside the glass on his wall. The thought of not being with him was more than I could handle.

I never questioned Tony, never demanded anything, and always made myself readily available. After the newness of the relationship started to wear off, I saw a change in him. He wasn't being consistent in seeing me. I caught him in lies and with other women. It brought about a rage in me that made me want to hurt him. I became extremely jealous. I had a suspicion he was with someone else and broke into his house and hid in the shower. They walked in and sat on the sofa. He turned the radio on. They talked for a few minutes, and I heard him say, "come on, let's go to the bedroom." My blood was boiling! Tears streamed down my face. As soon as they approached his bedroom door, I pulled back the shower curtain, "YOU SAID YOU LOVED ME!" I charged at him with the knife.

"What the hell you doing in here? How did you get in here?" Tony spoke with courage but was clearly frightened. The girl ran out the door. "Get out of my house!" Tony grabbed me by the arm, I dropped the knife. He was pulling me towards the door trying to get me to leave.

"I'm so sorry! I love you! Please forgive me! I wasn't going to hurt you!" I was screaming and crying and begging him to let me stay. I didn't know what had come over me. Tony wasn't hearing it. He told me it was over and made me leave. I promised myself if he took me back, I would never do that again. We couldn't stay away from each other more than a day before we were back making passionate love. This became our M.O. He cheated, I fought him, he kicked me out, and we'd make up.

The fights escalated to the cops being called and I would run before they got there. Tony's friend Nathan lived next door. His mother would always tell me, "Baby, ain't no man worth fighting over." Mrs. Dottie was a beautiful woman. She was independent, sophisticated, well-dressed, and she always smelled so good. She told me I could be anything I wanted to be. She told me whenever people doubted her ability to do something, it motivated her to want to do it even more just to prove them wrong. *"Please leave that boy alone,"* she said.

If only I had heeded Mrs. Dottie's advice.

Tony and I both knew our relationship needed to end, but we just couldn't leave each other alone. The longer he stayed away, the more I craved him. Just the thought of him or the mention of his name gave me chills. I saw Tony leave the club with a very attractive girl. All sorts of evil thoughts were running through my mind. I scared myself with what I was thinking. I knew for sure I was going to kill him, but I would have to kill her too. I broke into his house like always. The living room light was dimmed. The radio was on the Quiet Storm station playing all the love songs we'd made love to. The door to his bedroom was closed. I started hyperventilating at the thought of him making love to her the way he made love to me. I didn't know how I was going to carry out this double murder. *I don't have a gun. If I use a knife, it'll take too long.* I spotted the can of Crisco˚ oil on top of the stove. I tip-toed to the bedroom with the pot of hot grease and placed my ear against the door. I couldn't hear a sound. *There was no way she could be that quiet with Tony making love to her. Had they already had sex and fallen asleep?*

I turned the doorknob very slowly, prepared to fling the boiling hot grease directly on his face. Tony was in bed alone, mouth wide open snoring. *Where was the girl he left with? There wasn't enough time for her to have sex and leave.* I was relieved yet embarrassed. *He probably just gave her a ride home. Unless… he had sex with her somewhere else and then came home.* My mind went back and forth from still wanting to kill him to forgiving him. Watching him lay there reminded me of how much I truly loved him and could never hurt him.

Just as I was putting the pot of grease back on the stove, Tony walked in the kitchen. "What the hell are you doing in here? I thought I was dreaming I heard something. Is that grease! You mean to tell me you were going to…? I'm calling the police!"

"Tony! Please!!! I wasn't going to hurt you! I love you! Please don't do this to me! Please!"

"Get out of my house now!" He was serious.

"Okay! Okay! I'll leave." I walked towards the door, clenched my fist, swung around, and hit Tony in his right temple, causing his nose to bleed profusely. Tony ran out of the house. I was so terrified I couldn't move. Three police cars arrived, sirens wailing. The neighbors came outside in their pajamas and slippers. It wasn't until the officer handcuffed me that I realized I was in serious trouble. I saw the look of disappointment and sadness in Mrs. Dottie's eyes saying, I told you to leave that boy alone.

I was facing 35 years to life for attempted murder, assault, trespassing and breaking and entering. I went into a deep, dark depression thinking about what will happen to Kee-Kee. Maybe she's better off without me.

"Guard! Guard! This girl in here is cutting her wrists!" The guard came rushing in and snatched the Ace of spades card out of my hand and took me to the clinic. The cuts were only superficial and a ploy to get attention. I was released on my own recognizance bond and referred to a psychiatrist for suicidal evaluation.

I knew I needed help, and this was my chance to talk to someone who was nonjudgmental. He was a white man probably in his fifties, although his gray hair and beard lent him another ten years. He was short, a bit overweight and long overdue for a haircut and shave. He wasn't at all what I'd envisioned a psychiatrist to look like. The court ordered me to see him three times a week. My first visit was awkward, I barely talked. By the third visit, I was a little more relaxed and told him about my childhood abuse, promiscuity and multiple rapes. I felt like I was making some progress. About six visits in, I was feeling good about myself. I came late to one of my sessions and he was upset. "Do you realize you're fifteen minutes late?"

"I'm sorry, I applied for a job and the application took longer than I thought."

"Don't make excuses! If you want me to help you, you're going to have to be here on time, okay?"

"Yes, I understand," I told him.

"Now come here." He motioned for me to come behind his desk. I thought it was weird, but he was the professional and I thought it was part of the counseling. I walked over to his chair. "Turn around." He slapped my butt so hard it stung. "Do you realize you could go to jail for the rest of your life? Do you want me to help you get out of this trouble?"

"Yes sir."

He unzipped his pants. "Get on your knees." I went to court and the psychiatrist was there. He told the judge I had met all the requirements and the case was dismissed.

The betrayal of the psychiatrist almost took me over the edge, but I knew I had to keep going because it wasn't about me anymore. I had a little girl who needed me. I got a job waiting tables and met a family who took me in. Ironically, they were related to the girl who threw dirt in my hair. She was so ashamed when she saw me, but never apologized and I didn't bother telling her family what happened. I told Bert as soon as I saved enough money to get my own place, I would get Kee-Kee. "I don't give a damn. You can take her and stick her back up yo pussy" she said.

No matter how nasty she talked to me, I obeyed what the Bible said: "Honor thy father and mother."

It was six o'clock in the morning and the police came barging in and said I was under arrest for child support. I wasn't aware Bert was receiving public assistance for Kee-Kee and put me on child support, and I was in arrears for hundreds of dollars. She had also been receiving assistance for me and Shawn the entire time from when we were little. So, all the years we weren't allowed to stay with her, she barely fed us, she used the aid meant for her children to help a man instead. I hated her with every beat of my heart. After spending three days in jail, I was released. I went back to work, found an apartment, and got my daughter. I had worked at several fast-food places and was grateful to be working but wanted more.

Getting my G.E.D. was a priority. I went to see Mr. Andrews again and asked him to give me another chance. He agreed. He gave me the information, told me what books to study, and even paid for me to take the test. "You're going to have to find a way to get there." The test was being held twenty minutes away in Darlington County.

I assured Mr. Andrews I would get there. I studied day and night for the test. The day before, I asked everyone I knew with a car if they could take me to Darlington and no one would. I was determined to get there no matter what. The morning of the test, I was walking the streets at six o'clock, looking for a ride. If I didn't make it there promptly at eight o'clock. I wouldn't be allowed in. A friend of Tony's agreed to take me. "I can take you but you're going to have to find a ride back."

"That's fine. I will. I just need to get there." I told him. Ted got me there on time. I didn't have a dime to my name or anything to eat. We finished testing at two o'clock in the afternoon, and I had no idea how I was going to get back to Hartsville. I started walking down the highway. Thirty minutes later a truck driver asked me if I needed a ride. I hopped in the truck, and he took me straight to Hartsville.

The test results would be mailed in a couple of weeks. I checked the mail every day. Finally, the letter came. I ripped it open: PASSED! I screamed and jumped for joy! I was so proud of myself. After having dropped out of high school, night school, and having my books thrown in the trash, I did it. *Maybe one day I can go to college*, I told myself.

Tony and I called it quits for good. The love was still there and would always be, but we loved each other enough to let it go. He and his girlfriend got married and had baby. At the end of the summer, I packed up and moved to Columbia.

CHAPTER 4

It is not selfish to put yourself first when you create your life. When you take time for yourself, you make everything around you better.

- Toni Morrison

- Bleach on Colored Clothes -

"Where are you going to college, Joretta?" The question caught me off guard. Gail's friend Nancy managed a women's clothing store and gave me a job. Three girls were all discussing what college they were going to attend. I was already uncomfortable being in social settings due to my lack of social skills.

"I haven't decided what I want to do yet."

The white girls were from two-parent homes who lived in upscale neighborhoods. This was just a summer job until they left for college. For me, it was to support me and my daughter. It took four years to get my G.E.D., so college wasn't even in my thought process. I was just happy to put Hartsville behind me. Nancy was very nice to me and extremely patient even though it took me forever to learn basic things, like counting the drawer and batching out the credit card machine. Once I was fully trained, she gave me the responsibility of opening and closing the store. Then came a small promotion and a pay increase. It wasn't a lot, but enough to pay rent and utilities. And I was lucky enough to find an apartment within walking distance.

Now that I was in Columbia for the second time, it was different, because the first time I was pregnant and only left the house to go to my doctor's appointments.

I was able to see Linda more often. She would stop by my job sometimes to see me or pick me up on the weekends and take me to her house. Her home was immaculate and beautifully decorated. The deep melodic sounds of Oleta Adams, Minnie Riperton and Randy Crawford could be heard from the driveway. It was a joy being around her, except when her boyfriend was around, who wasn't a nice person.

I could tell he was insecure, controlling and very possessive. I noticed how tense Linda was around him. I wondered what she saw in him because if there were ever two people who were incompatible, they were. His long, permed hair and Superfly wardrobe of flashy suits and hats diminished Linda's chic designer labels. Linda was refined, beautiful, intelligent and graceful. He was deceptive, manipulative and opportunistic.

Nancy was transferred to Atlanta. I was disappointed she was leaving and no longer wanted to work there. I found another retail job across town and an apartment within walking distance. Linda came to see me and recognized someone she knew. "Jo, I know him!" Pointing in the direction of the man wearing a Do-rag. "That's Leon! He's so nice! He used to roommate with my friend Bonnie. He'll do anything for you—take you to the store and even watch Kee-Kee. He's a really nice guy."

Linda sounded as if she were suggesting we date. Dating was the furthest thing from my mind. It was in a man's best interest and mine that I keep my distance. Leon was meticulously shining the tires on his freshly waxed candy apple red Nissan 300z. The sultry sound of Sade blasting from his car drowned out Linda calling his name.

"Heeyy! How you doin? I didn't see you over there. What you doin out here?" Leon asked Linda.

"This is my little sister Jo. She lives out here. I was telling her I knew you and what a nice guy you were." Leon was just over 5'9, with an average build of about 180. His skin was a dark charcoal brown, and he had a round face with small eyes and deep forehead lines that moved when he talked. Leon and I exchanged hellos.

"If you need anythang let me know." The sincerity of his statement was comforting.

Months after being on the job, things got tough. After paying the rent and utilities, I barely had enough for food. I desperately needed more income, but the only way to generate more money was to either get a better-paying job or a second job. The latter was more realistic, because other than the restaurant industry, retail was the only thing I was qualified to do. I got a part-time job at Pizza Hut® across the street from my full-time job.

I met a lady who lived in my complex. She worked for D.S.S. (Department of Social Services), was a Christian and had a little girl close to Kee-Kee's age. This was the ideal person and she offered to let Kee-Kee come over after school and stay with them for free. Her husband was a truck driver and was hardly ever at home, so I felt comfortable with Kee-Kee being there.

I worked from 6 pm until 11 pm. And even the money from that job wasn't enough, I was exhausted all the time. I wasn't spending any time with Kee-Kee, and she was complaining about not wanting to stay at the lady's house. I ignored her complaints and blew it off as whining and demanded she continue to go over there. I was having anxiety and was frustrated that nothing seemed to be going right. This was not what I'd expected. I wanted to do well so I could go back and show Bert and all the other abusers they were wrong about me.

"Jo, I'm going to Hartsville this weekend. You wanna go?" I hadn't seen or talked to Bert, so when Linda asked, I was eager to go. Linda and I didn't converse much. I was still getting to know her and was hoping she'd ask me what happened to me growing up, but she never did. And I didn't volunteer to tell. Maybe it was best to let it go. There was no one at Mr. Billy's house when we got there. Mr. Billy was up the street at the bar drinking and smoking a cigarette. "Y'all looking for Bert? I'll show you way she at." He got in the back seat and directed Linda to a motel room. Bert was happy to see Kee-Kee but never acknowledged me.

I gasped at the sight of her. Her cheeks were hollow, eyes haunting, her face was badly mutilated, and as people would often say, "she couldn't have weighed a hundred pounds soak and wet with bricks in her pocket."

She said Billy had beat her with a hammer. Linda tried to get her to go back with us, but she didn't want to leave. I couldn't understand what would make a woman stay with a man who brutally beats her. A few weeks later, Linda asked me to ride with her to Hartsville again. She said we would leave early Saturday morning and was just going for the day. One of my coworkers agreed to let Kee-Kee stay with her.

"Jo, do you know how to drive? I need to polish my nails before we get to Hartsville." I told her I could, knowing I had never been behind the wheel of a car. I always watched her when she drove, and it seemed easy if I stayed in my lane. Linda pulled over and I got in the driver's seat. I pressed the gas and slammed on the brakes so hard, our heads jerked. "JO!!! I thought you said you knew how to drive! Damn! I hope I don't have whiplash!"

"I'm sorry, I guess I need a little more practice." We laughed and I got back on the passenger's side. Linda didn't tell me who she was going to see, and I didn't ask. I waited in the car while she went inside to visit. She came out after several hours and we headed back to Columbia. It was just starting to get dark when we pulled in the driveway. Her boyfriend Mickey was standing on the porch. I could tell he was upset from the look on his face. I also noticed how nervous Linda was.

We walked in the house, he and Linda went to her bedroom and closed the door, and I went in the other bedroom. I got the same feeling in the pit of my stomach I got right before Howard beat Bert. I could hear them fussing. It got louder, then I heard Linda scream, "Jo! Call 911!" I picked up the phone and Linda ran in the room where I was. He was right behind her. He snatched the phone out my hand and out of the wall and threw it across the room. He grabbed me and Linda and threw us to the floor. He pinned us against the wall with his left arm, while punching us with his right fist like a professional boxer.

I held my head down so he couldn't get to my face. We were crying and begging for him to stop. "Imma kill both of you bitches!" He had such a strong hold on us, we couldn't break free. With every blow, the warmth of Linda's blood spattered on me like drops of rain. I knew if I didn't do something he was going to kill us. Whatever I decided to do, I couldn't miss. I had a flashback of Mrs. Rose squeezing Mr. Pee-Wee's balls. I grabbed Mickey's balls and twisted them with all my might. "You Bitch!" He let go. I ran to the next-door neighbor's house and banged on the door.

"Help! Please Help!" Mickey was just a few feet away from grabbing me when the man opened the door, and he ran. I looked back, Linda was crawling out of the apartment, her face bloody and swollen. "Thank you! Jo. Thank you!"

Almost every bone in Linda's face was broken. Mickey was arrested the next day and Linda was granted an emergency restraining order. It felt like I was reliving what I had gone through with Bert all over again. I thought this type of domestic violence only happened in poor, uneducated families with alcohol and drug abuse problems.

Linda was educated, middle class (other than an occasional drink of Crème Liqueur) she was an outstanding person.

Gail, Jean and Wade came to Linda's aid. She revealed to us she had been a battered woman for many years. It was disheartening to hear her stories of how Mickey checked the mileage on the car whenever she returned home from work or grocery shopping. He intercepted her mail and stole checks and money from her. Every day she came home from work, he examined her underwear and vagina to see if she had been with anyone. He told her if he couldn't have her, no one else could. She said there were times he had beaten her for so long she wished he would kill her. Maybe if I hadn't been with her that night he would have. She said that time was the last time and started preparing to end the relationship. Her job approved a transfer to Atlanta.

A week before her move she came by my job to see me and was so excited about starting her new life. Days went by and no one heard from her. A missing person report was filed. A couple of weeks later, her body was discovered in the trunk of her car. For whatever reason, she entrusted herself to be with him again and he made sure that no one else would have her. That was the first time I had someone so close to me die and in such a tragic manner. I thought we would all grow old and die peacefully in our sleep. Linda's death was unshakeable and furthered my intense hatred toward men.

"You want a ride?" Leon was showing all thirty-two of his white teeth.

"Thanks, but I'm just going to Food Lion˚."

"That's a long walk. I don't mind taking you." It was a bit of a hike, but I was used to doing it. And I didn't want Leon to think I was needy. "I'm sorry about what happened to Linda. I'm glad his ass got twenty years in prison. His ass shoulda got life."

"Thank you. I can't believe it's been three months since she died. It seems like yesterday." Leon must have sensed it bothered me to talk about it and changed the subject. "Why your boyfriend got you out here walking to the store?"

Okay Leon, if you wanna know if I have a boyfriend, just ask. "I don't have a boyfriend." "You mean to tell me somebody as good looking as you ain't got nobody."

"Nope, and I don't want one." I didn't ask him if he had a girlfriend because I didn't care. If we keep it cordial, we'll be just fine. However, our cordiality was very brief; we went from having casual conversations to having casual sex. It had been a while and I needed to relieve some bottled-up anger and stress. I told myself I wouldn't repeat this same pattern again. But this time was different. I wasn't being forced. He was a nice guy and I had built up a resistance to becoming emotionally attached. I just need to stay in control. Leon came over late at night several times a week after work.

The rules were: no kissing, cuddling or spending the night. One-night things got a little extreme (nothing like Tony), but it was a little more passionate and lasted longer. We both fell asleep immediately afterward. This was not supposed to happen. I wanted to be clear it was only sex, nothing more.

That better not be a Jehovah's Witness at my door this early in the morning. I knew very few people and couldn't imagine who it could be. The lady was short, with rectangular wire-rimmed glasses. The look on her face was not that of a Jehovah's Witness. Before I could tell her I wasn't interested in whatever she was selling, she asked, "Is Leon in there? I'm his mother and his girlfriend Cynthia is waiting for him at his apartment."

This was not how I wanted to meet anyone's mother. And it wasn't how I wanted to find out about Leon's girlfriend. "Yes ma'am, he's here."

"Leon! Wake up! Yo Mama want you." Leon jumped up disoriented. Then looked at me with dazed bloodshot eyes. "My mama?"

"Yeah, yo mama."

"I'll talk to you about this later." He said as they were leaving.

"Don't even worry about it," I told him. I heard his mother scold him about cheating on his girlfriend. Finding out about Leon's girlfriend made it that much easier for me to not get my feelings involved. I was at work and my friend Ina told me she had a dream about fish. Dreaming about fish is an Old Wives tale that meant someone close was pregnant.

"It's not me. It must be you, Joretta." I quickly dismissed it even though the month was almost over, and I hadn't seen my period. Ina bought a pregnancy test and there they were: the "double lines." I wasn't sure how Leon was going to take the news. He didn't have any children and we never discussed whether he wanted any or not. And I sure as hell didn't need another baby.

Without hesitation, he said, "You need to have an abortion."

"I've never had an abortion, don't know anyone who has, and don't know where to get one. I was taught in church that having an abortion was murder. If I did, I would surely go to hell when I die and see the baby as punishment by God."

"Ask Ina, she might know where you can go." Leon was unemotional and very matter of fact. "I ain't ready for no lil crumb snatcher rat now. You know I got a girlfriend. What Imma tell her?" Leon pressed me every day about it until Ina found a place. He didn't even have the decency to go with me. He gave me the money to pay for it and asked Ina if she could take me. I was angry at myself for allowing this to happen again and thinking Leon wasn't like all the others. He was hard-working, quiet and easygoing. A simple man from low country South Carolina who spoke with the unique "Geechee[3]" accent. He took pride in his clothes. When he wore jogging suits, his sneakers had to match. His jeans had to have a heavy starch and sharp crease. Shirts always tucked in with a belt. The waves in his hair were accelerated by Murray's Hair Dressing Pomade®, which left a subtle vanilla scent wherever he went.

The day of the abortion Ina couldn't stay with me. I wasn't given any information on what to expect. The clinic was in a sketchy part of town in a building that looked abandoned. It was cold, dark and dreary. The antiquated furniture and medical equipment looked inoperative. The older

---

[3] Geechee, known by their more formal name, Gullah Geechee, are descendants of West Africa. Due to their isolation on islands off the Carolinas and Georgia, their language, culture and food are set apart from that of southern or African American, and have more in common with their West African roots.

white man who assumed the role of the doctor looked more like the man who cleaned fish down at the fish market rather than someone equipped to perform that type of procedure. The only question he asked was if I had cash, then he gave me a pill to take. I removed my skirt and laid on the cold steel table. A dingy sheet was placed over the lower part of my abdomen. "Put your feet in the stir-ups." He inserted a cold sharp object into my vagina. He poked and prodded causing my buttocks to raise off the table. "Be still" he said.

"It Hurts!" A lady came over and held my knees in place. I let out a blood-curdling scream! "SOMEBODY PLEASE HELP ME! OH, GOD PLEASE HELP ME! IT HURTS SO BAD! PLEASE STOP!" I dug my nails in the side of the table, my body trembled from shock and the freezing cold temperature. He scraped, pulled, picked and tugged as if he was extracting a wisdom tooth.

After what seemed like thirty minutes of unendurable pain, it was finally over. The lady assisted me off the table all bloody and barely able to walk. She walked me out the back door to an alley where Ina was waiting. "You don't look good. What in the hell did they do in there? You need to go to the doctor!"

"No, I just want to go home." The physical pain and scars took weeks to heal, but the mental and emotional scars never went away. Days after my abortion, the clinic was shut down for practicing without a license in unsafe and unsanitary conditions. Aborted fetuses were also discovered, thrown in the dumpster like everyday trash.

Leon had the audacity to ask me how it was. "How do think you think having a baby scraped from my uterus was!?" To him it was no different than going to the dentist. And he even had the nerve to allude to us having sex again. I hated him for putting me through that. I immediately got on birth control because I never wanted to go through that again.

Being in that apartment and in that area reminded me too much of Linda and what I had just gone through. I no longer wanted to live there. I sent Kee-Kee to live with Gail in Atlanta until I could do better. I changed jobs and apartments again. Columbia isn't a huge city but big enough to not have to see the same people every day. Shawn was finally released from prison and came to stay with me. He'd spent most of his teenage years in juvenile detention and resorted to doing more serious crimes that landed him in the penitentiary.

He had his own set of issues that hadn't been dealt with. We were all we had, and I tried to be the mother that neither one of us had. My wish for him was to get a job, find a nice girl, get married and have children. It was going to be challenging considering, neither of us knew how to drive and he didn't have any job skills. I walked to the store and who do I see in the apartment complex, Leon. "How you doing?" he asked.

"I'm fine."

"You live out here now?"

"Yes, what are you doing out here?" I asked him.

"A partner of mine live out here." Leon and his friends were gathered in the parking lot drinking beer. Shawn would fit right in. Leon told me he was working at the Army base painting. I introduced him to Shawn, and they hit it off right away. He got Shawn a job that he got fired from after working one month. Shawn never tried to find another job and decided he would go back to Hartsville. Leon and I started having sex again. He wasn't helping me and was still with his girlfriend and sharing an apartment with his brother. I told him I needed to concentrate on getting my daughter. Gail agreed I should come to Atlanta and stay with her. My job allowed me to transfer. I told Leon I was leaving. I hated Columbia and the entire state of South Carolina for all the terrible things it had done to me.

CHAPTER 5

With everything that has happened to you, you can either feel sorry for yourself or treat what has happened as a gift. Everything is either an opportunity to grow or an obstacle to keep you from growing.

- Wayne Dyer

- Bleach on Colored Clothes -

"Joretta, exit the stage. Joretta, please exit the stage." Those words were echoed by the D.J. every Friday night. "Girl, get yo behind off that stage and let's go." Keisha and I met at work and became instant friends. She had just moved to Atlanta from Alabama. She worked in Loss Prevention where she was responsible for catching shoplifters. A position not too many females were hired for due to the nature of the job. But Keisha wasn't intimidated by that. She was 6 feet tall and had muscular arms and legs. I saw her once apprehend and wrestle a big burly guy to the ground for stealing.

She had a tom-boyish look at work, but when we went out at night, she was a girly girl. She had a short, sexy haircut, polished pink nails, sparkling lip gloss and miniskirts to show off her beautiful long, mocha-toned, legs. Nightlife in Atlanta was electrifying. I was just working and staying at home, so Gail suggested I get out more. Keisha told me about a club in College Park. She picked me up Friday night in her 1980 tan-colored Ford Pinto. I remembered how impressed I was with how well she could drive a stick shift and I didn't know how to drive a car at all.

As soon as I walked in the club, a man took me by the hand and led me to the dance floor. I got on the stage and didn't sit down until the music slowed down. From that night on, Keisha and I became regulars. Everyone from the bartender, bouncer, staff and D.J. knew our names. If we missed a Friday night (which was rare), the following Friday, someone would ask, "what happened to y'all last Friday?" We closed the club down every time. The lights came on and I would still be on the stage, until the D.J. told me to get off.

"What you doing Saturday night? Keisha asked. "We're going to have to check out this other club." Keisha was single and didn't have any children, so she was free to come and go as she pleased.

Even though Gail said I needed to get out, I didn't want to take advantage. Gail reminded me, "You've been going out almost every Friday night. You know you have a child to take care of. Go ahead, just don't make it a habit." Saturday became a regular party night as well. And it didn't stop there. I was partying four nights out of the week. Frozen Paradise on Sunday, Fat Tuesday on Tuesday, The Club on Friday, The Omega "Frat House" and/ or Talisman on Saturday.

When Gail refused to watch Kee-Kee, I waited until she went to sleep and sneaked out. She was probably afraid I was going to get pregnant again. I had met several guys my age who would have made great boyfriends, but it was awkward for me because I didn't know how to be a girlfriend. All my sexual encounters with men were either forced or long-term one-night stands.

Gail was taking me to work on her way to work and picking me up on her way home. It wasn't out of her way, but I could see it was starting to inconvenience her. The tension was so thick, the fifteen-minute drive felt like thirty. "What are your plans on moving out?" I didn't have an answer because I didn't have any plans. I had ideas about what I wanted, but I didn't know how to go about executing them. How was I supposed to get an apartment, a car (that I couldn't drive), pay for afterschool care (because Kee-Kee was too young to stay by herself), pay utilities, food, etc. on a retail job making minimum wage of $4.25 per hour? After I didn't respond, she responded by saying, "I'll start looking around for you. I know they have some low-income places somewhere." Gail didn't want to throw me out, but the environment she created made it uncomfortable to live in.

The stress I felt from being unwelcomed, I took out on Kee-Kee. I don't recall the first time I yelled at her or hit her, but I vividly remember the morning I got angry at her for taking too long to get dressed for school. I was afraid she'd missed the bus and I started choking her and tried to throw her out the window. My little nephew, who was just a few years older than Kee-Kee, stopped me. I deeply regretted it, but I never comforted her or told her I was sorry. I felt horrible and told myself I would never do that again.

Living in a big city without personal transportation is almost impossible unless you live on the bus line. Gail lived on the outskirts and took another job farther away from where I worked. I had two choices: find a place of my own close to my job or quit and find another job close to where she was moving. Her friend Nancy was managing another clothing store close to Gail's new place and gave me a job. The pay was a little more than I was making at my previous job but getting to work was still an issue. I had to take a taxi that took fifty percent of my earnings to get to and from work.

Gail implied that I needed to learn how to drive as if I didn't know that already. There were a lot of things I should have known how to do. Jean had already graduated from nursing school and got married. Her husband said he would teach me how to drive. I got my permit, and he took me out every Saturday morning to a huge parking lot to practice. After months of practicing, he said I was ready to try for my license. "I think you'll do fine on everything, except parallel parking. I don't know what you're going to do when they ask you to parallel park, because you ran over the cones every time." The instructor seemed to be agitated. We drove a few blocks and when we got back to the parking lot, he asked me to parallel park. He gave me three tries and I failed three times. "You know if those were cars, you just hit them? I'm going to give you your license today, but please learn how to parallel park!"

Somehow Keisha and I lost contact when Gail moved, and we never hung out again. Maybe that was Gail's way of keeping me from going out so much. I always sensed she thought Keisha was a bad influence on me. On the contrary, she was a nice person. We were just two girls from the country having a good time in what we thought at the time was this big city.

From time to time, Gail would introduce me to some of her coworkers' sisters who were my age, but we didn't click. One of her coworkers had a nephew my age and suggested we go out. Tony offered to take me to see Whitney Houston. I was a huge fan and was elated. This would be my first concert and first date. I got my hair done and Nancy helped me pick out a cute outfit. He said to be ready at six so we could grab something to eat first. I was dressed at 5:30 dancing in front of the mirror to "I'm Your Baby Tonight." I couldn't wait for him to see how cute I looked. Six o'clock came but no Tony.

Thirty minutes went by, and he still wasn't there. I started to feel uneasy, but I knew we still had time to make the concert even if we didn't stop to eat. "Maybe he's stuck in traffic." Gail could see I was getting apprehensive. Three hours later I was still sitting on the sofa. "Jo, I'm so sorry. I can't believe he stood you up."

I knew at 6:30 he wasn't coming, but I couldn't move. I went to my room and bawled my eyes out. Reminded all over again of the day I waited for Bert to come, and she never did.

Why he didn't show up, I would never know. I never talked to him again. If Gail talked to his aunt, she didn't tell me. Gail was offered another position a few months later and wanted to be closer to work. There was an abundance of retail jobs close to her new place, which made it easy for me to find one. I went to Rich's Department Store and was hired on the spot. It was also on the bus line, which solved my transportation problem.

The store was beautiful, the people were friendly, and I could take the bus to and from work, so I didn't have to inconvenience Gail. I figured six months of savings would get me a down payment on a car so I could look for a better-paying job and find a place to live. Well, there was my plan and Gail's plan. She had planned to buy a house soon and asked me to move. She broke the news to me the same day Magic Johnson shocked the world with his HIV announcement.

I made a failed attempt at telling Gail what happened to me growing up. It was one of the most disengaging and unemotional conversations I'd ever had. Not that I was looking for pity, but a little empathy would have done some good. It was like asking to borrow money from someone you're afraid to ask; and when you finally get the courage to do so, they say no, and you regret having asked.

I don't know how Kee-Kee managed to cope with moving from place to place. Constantly having to change schools, but she didn't miss a beat and took everything in stride. Kee-Kee reminded me a lot of myself when I was her age. She was very much attuned to what was going on around her. She could sense I was in turmoil and was careful not to do anything that might contribute to it but looking for a way to fix it.

My biggest need was finding someone to look after her when school was out so I wouldn't have to rush to the bus stop every day. The longer I could stay at work, the more money I could make and find a place. Everything was timed to the second; catch the bus to get Kee-Kee, take her to Gail's house, and take the bus back to work to finish my shift. Kee-Kee introduced me to a girl who was waiting with her at the bus stop. "Mom, this is my friend Tasha, she said her mommy will watch me." And just like that, Kee-Kee had solved my childcare problem. She had already told Tasha's mom about my situation. When Kee-Kee was three years old, older people used to say she had been here before.

Jesse had relocated to Atlanta from Missouri one year prior. She was in her early sixties and had six adult children of her own. She adopted Tasha when she was two years old. My first impression of Jesse was questionable. She had a scowl on her face. Her Jheri curl had more Jheri than curl, and she barely smiled. Her tiny eyes peered at me over her bifocals as if I was being X-rayed. Neither one of us knew anything about the other, but we trusted our instincts. I moved in, Tasha and Kee-Kee got along great, and Jesse treated me like I was one of her daughters. I found a better-paying job managing a boutique. On Sundays when the bus didn't run Jesse let me drive her car to work.

We ate at Wendy's® every Friday night, hot wings from the Three Dollar Café on Saturdays, and Krispy Kreme® on Sunday only when the hot light was on.

She was like the mother I never had. I looked forward to her scrumptious Chicken Cacciatore dinner on Sundays. Not a day went by without getting a call from Jesse when I was at work. Her greeting was always the same, "Hey babe! How's your day going?" Just hearing those words brought me so much joy. It took a while before I shared my past with her, and she shared a traumatic experience she had when she was a little girl and said I was the first person she ever told. Jesse was very supportive and told me not to be in a hurry about moving. I had given myself a year to save money and get a car before moving out.

My tax refund that year was $1500.00. A preacher sold me a 1982 Burgundy Cutlass Supreme for the exact amount. I was so proud of myself and couldn't wait to drive it to work. The car didn't make it two blocks before it started backfiring and smoking. Jesse had it towed to a repair shop and the mechanic told me it was a lemon and would cost more to fix it than it was worth. He said the best thing I could do was to take it to a junkyard. I didn't even have the car for 24 hours. Jesse asked the preacher to give me my money back, but he refused. He said it was an "as is" sale.

Later that afternoon at work, a man came in the boutique, and we started talking. The subject of cars came up and I told him what happened to my car and started crying. He said to me, "Bless that car and ask God to get you a brand new one." "Okay," I said. All the while thinking to myself, yeah, right. I've been asking God to do a lot of things and he hasn't listened. God is going to do what God wants to do.

Jesse loved the Arsenio Hall show and we watched it every Friday night. "I'm thinking about trading my car in. You wanna go with me in the morning to look at a car? You might see something you like too."

"I don't have any money or credit to buy a car, Jesse."

"It don't cost nothing to look" she said. We went to the Toyota dealership and Jesse settled on a Blue Toyota Camry. There was a little Red Toyota Tercel that caught my eye, and the size was just right. Jesse asked the salesman what the minimum down payment, terms and conditions were. He said they had a first-time buyer's program and if I could put $1500.00 down, he could get me in the car. Without hesitation, Jesse wrote him a check for the down payment, and we drove off the lot in our new cars. The relationship with Jesse felt almost too good to be true.

She never gave me a reason to question her kindness, but every now and then, thoughts about her sincerity and motives crept up, causing me to cast doubt. Several books I had read about being a child of alcoholics talked about the impact it had later in life. Lack of trust being one of the characteristics of Adult Children of Alcoholics (ACOS).

Chaos and instability had been a constant theme in my life; stability and normalcy felt odd. There were times when out of nowhere I would have bouts of anger and depression. Jesse was a talker and sometimes I didn't want to be bothered. I felt guilty for feeling that way, so I'd sit and endure listening to her talk endlessly when I wanted to be alone. I acknowledged I had a problem and needed help, but I didn't know where or how to get it. I thought by ignoring it, it would go away, only to realize it exacerbated it.

During my research, I found a support group for ACOS. The meeting was held at a catholic church in the ritzy part of Roswell. I thought I must have been in the wrong place. All the women were white, very elegant and accomplished. They didn't look like they belonged there and being shunned by them let me know I didn't belong there either.

I sat through the meeting because I wanted to hear their stories of what it was like for them. Nothing they said compared to what I had gone through. One lady complained about her nanny having to take care of her because her father worked too much, and her mother was passed out all the time from drinking. All the women were college graduates who came from well-to-do families or had married well. I sat in a circle listening to one after the other complain about a lifestyle that I would have gladly exchanged for mine.

When it was my turn, I declined to share my story. There was nothing this meeting could help me with. My relationship with Jesse grew stronger and closer. Her daughters came to visit and welcomed me with open arms. We drove to Savannah to visit her son and his family. "You don't have a boyfriend, Jo?" Jesse asked, followed by her silly grin.

"No, I don't. I was wondering when you were going to ask." I replied. I was still in touch with Leon. He was a nice guy, and I knew he would always be in my corner, but I hadn't forgiven him for the abortion. This was my chance to get on my feet and I wasn't going to take Jesse for granted. She always made it clear that I could stay with her as long as I needed to. We continued our daily check-ins and weekend rituals. We had Wendy's® Friday night like always and later that night right before Arsenio came on Jesse said she had a taste for some hot wings. "Do you feel like going to the Three Dollar Café and get us some wings?"

"So does that mean we'll have wings again tomorrow night too?" I asked.

We both laughed and said, "I don't mind." Jesse sat in the bed eating her wings and I sat in the chair right beside her. We laughed and talked about the show and other things. I was so tired; I could barely keep my eyes open. I saw Jesse nodding and I started to tiptoe out of the room.

"Where are you going. You thought I was sleep, huh?" We laughed, and I sat back down. Jesse's voice got quiet, and I looked over at her and could tell she was sound asleep. I carefully slid the piece of chicken out of her hand and put her plate on the nightstand. I'd better leave her glasses on and the lamp because she'll wake up and tell me to sit back down. She'll wake up in the middle of the night and take her glasses off and turn off the light. Tasha ran in my room, "Jo, wake up. I can't get mama to wake up!" Jesse was always the first one up on Saturday mornings.

Disoriented, thinking I was dreaming, "What do you mean 'you can't wake her up?'" I jumped out of bed and as soon as I entered her room I knew. She was in the exact same position I'd left her in. Her glasses still on her face, the lamp and TV still on. Her mouth was slightly opened. I held my hand against her mouth to see if I could feel her breath.

"Jesse!!! Jesse!!! Please wake up!!!" I had my hands on her shoulders shaking her, begging her to wake up. "No!! No!! No!! No!!! No!!!!!!" I screamed to the top of my lungs and collapsed on the floor. The paramedics came and my last vison of her was her body covered with a white sheet on a stretcher. Her children came down and like all families, they walked through the house claiming items like they were at a yard sale. They argued with each other about what Jesse would have wanted them to have. They made sure to let me know the bedroom furniture I paid for was all I was entitled to. I didn't want or ask for anything, except for a green and white piggy bank in the shape of a bunny I named Jesse. It was on her nightstand, and I said to her one day, "this is a cute little bunny, it has a nose just like yours. I'm going to call her Jesse." She agreed and thought it was funny. Her children gave me two weeks to move out. I packed everything that would fit in my Tercel, and Kee-Kee and I was on to the next adventure.

CHAPTER 6

Refuse to inherit dysfunction. Learn new ways of living instead of repeating what you lived through.

- Thema Davis

- Bleach on Colored Clothes -

The three apartments I applied for denied me. The complex where Jesse lived would only approve me if I paid three months' rent upfront. There was no way I could come up with that. I now understood what Bert must have felt. Scared and frustrated not knowing how she was going to provide for her children with no resources. I had a job and a car and was still afraid. I sat in my car in front of the leasing office and thought of how much more I could accomplish if I didn't have Kee-Kee. Not that I didn't want her. I was terrified of being a mother.

"Glen?" What are you doing out here?"

"I live out here," he said.

"Did you move out here?" he asked. I told him what happened, and I was waiting for Kee-Kee to get off the bus. Glen was Gail's ex-coworker. He and some of her other coworkers came over a few times and talked I.T. jargon. There were a couple of hours before school was out, so Glen invited me in to kill time. The sex was over faster than it took to take our clothes off and get in the bed. It was something weird about having sex with a grown man whose feet stopped at my ankles and a penis the size of a cigarette lighter. All in all, he was a nice intelligent man.

Glen let me stay with him with no strings attached. The hours I worked were no longer conducive to Kee-Kee's school schedule and it was only a matter of time before I would have to quit. I saw a "now hiring" sign at the Sizzler® Restaurant and went inside. The waitress told the manager to hire me, and he did.

Deborah had a wonderful personality. She was energetic, funny and easy to talk to. She had a daughter the same age as Kee-Kee. I told her about my temporary stay at Glen's and she invited me to come live with her. Kee-Kee had to change schools again. And like always, she rolled with the punches. My conversations with God were to not let anything else happen. My anxiety had heightened, and I was riddled with fear and worry. I'd inherited it from Bert. Kee-Kee was outside playing with the children from the neighborhood. She came in the house limping and crying that her foot was hurting. "What's wrong with you?"

"I was running and fell."

"Why in the hell were you out there running around? Why couldn't you just stand your ass still!"

"We were playing hide 'n seek, and I tripped over a rock and fell."

"I tell you what, you gon hide 'n seek your ass to school tomorrow," I told her.

"It hurts mom. I can't walk on it." Kee-Kee said through lots of crying.

"Girl, ain't nothing wrong with your foot! You get on my fucking nerves! Shut Up and stop crying!" When she came home from school her foot was so swollen, I had to take her to the emergency room. The x-rays showed her foot was broken. Instead of apologizing and consoling her, I used it to cuss her out and beat her for having an accident. I accused her of trying to sabotage me. I remember telling Bert I would never treat my daughter the way she treated me. Here I was acting more like Bert than she was herself. I felt the adrenaline rush and rage. The way I projected my voice and spoke bitterly from the bottom of my belly, stressing every syllable in every cuss word I could think of. That's why Bert's words hurt so much, they were spoken with so much venom and passion ... and I had mastered it. I never felt okay abusing Kee-Kee. I knew it was weakness. I justified it by comparing how I treated her to how I saw other mothers treat their children worse than I did. I didn't want to admit I was abusing my child. There is no one more forgiving than a child. I could beat Kee-Kee one minute and the next minute she loved on me like nothing happened. I once heard a man say, "The most dangerous place for a child is with his mother because she has total control." Truer words were never spoken.

Waiting tables at The Sizzler® resolved my childcare problems, but it wasn't enough money to afford a place. Staying at Deborah's was fine but I wanted a place of my own. I mentioned to one of my regular customers I was looking for a place to stay. She made a call to a friend of hers, who was the director of Marietta Housing Authorities. A week later, I moved in.

I had my reservations about moving in the projects. Clay Homes was located at The Marietta Square across from Cobb County Courthouse and Marietta Police Department, so I felt safe.

The third-floor apartment was in a building with all elderly people. The grounds were well-kept, and I never saw anyone loitering. I was able to transfer my job with Sizzler®, which was two miles away. I gave myself a year to stay there and devised a plan of all the things I was going to do: go back to school and save enough money to pay a year's rent upfront when I moved out. I had to make sure not to get complacent or become a statistic, which was easy to do when your rent is forty dollars a month, which included utilities. Although public housing was designed as a steppingstone, I could see how some people got trapped. They made it easy to stay and almost impossible to leave. Kee-Kee had made friends with a little girl at the last school she attended and was spending most weekends with her which allowed me the opportunity to work longer hours.

The more I worked the less time I was at home. I was cordial with the neighbors but kept to myself to avoid falling into the project mentality. Waiting tables became more than a job, it helped with my extreme shyness and provided the income criteria needed to stay in my apartment. And just maybe introduce me to my husband, even though I vowed I'd never marry. I was terrified of marrying a man like my father and traumatized of being a wife like my mother. There was also a deep-rooted fear that made its appearance every time I met someone who was different from what I was familiar with.

If they were college educated and from a nice home, I didn't think I was good enough. If they were less smart, I was comfortable. If I stayed away from men who consumed too much alcohol and weren't abusive, I'd be okay.

Leon was coming to see me periodically, but we hadn't made a commitment. I made a few trips to Hartsville to check on Bert, Howard and Shawn. Nothing had changed. Bert was still getting drunk and beaten by Mr. Billy. Howard was still moving from porch to porch and Shawn had moved in with his girlfriend and her mother.

Every time I went home, I saw Tony. And every time we made love, it always felt like the very first time. We were still very much in love with each other. "You know it liked da kill me when you left. All you had to do was say you wanted us to be together and I swear I woulda been yours. All you got to do now is say it and I'm gone. Can I come to Georgia and see you some time?"

"I don't think your wife would like that. And you're just talking. You're already married and even if you weren't, it wouldn't work because I'll never move back to Hartsville, and you'll never leave." We kissed and said our goodbyes. It was hard leaving Tony, but I left knowing I had a chance to experience what it felt like to love and be loved. It was also hard leaving Howard and Bert in their condition. I wished there was more I could do to help them. All I ever wanted to do was become successful so I could take care of them.

Chattahoochee Technical College was offering a program for single moms to go back to school. I met with an advisor and decided on Business Management. The plan was to complete two years and enroll in a four-year university. My classes were going well and I had made a couple of friends. My advisor told me about another program at an all-female private liberal arts college she thought would be good for me once I completed my two years.

During my homeless teenage years, I kept a journal of everything that had happened to me for the book I was going to write one day. My advisor and I looked at the programs offered. "They offer Business Management. You could continue with that," she said.

"What about English?" I asked. "They offer English Literature Creative Writing."

"Maybe I should take that. I want to write a book."

"I think you should stick to Business Management. You'd have to be smart to write a book. I know you read very well but you're not a writer." I heard what she said, and I felt what she said. Her words stung the same as when Bert told me I was stupid and when Harry told me school had played out. Maybe she was right. I didn't feel smart, even though I was passing my classes. The only reason I enrolled in Business Management was because there was very little math.

Shelia was one of the ladies I'd met at school. She was a caregiver for an elderly lady and needed someone else to help her, so she asked if I'd be interested. The lady required 24-hour care and Shelia had been staying with her seven days a week around the clock. "I really need a break. The money is good, but I can't enjoy it because I'm there all the time," she said.

We agreed I would come in on Monday mornings and stay until Thursday evening. Shelia would work Thursday through Monday. The owner of the agency agreed to pay me $700.00 a week in cash. I accepted the job assuming Kee-Kee could stay there with me, but she couldn't.

"She can stay with me. I'll take her to school and pick her up." Shelia brushed her blonde hair with her fingers away from her face. Her sky-blue eyes said she knew from my facial expression that she had crossed her boundaries. Shelia had two teenage daughters who stayed with their father. She had been a homemaker for years but had recently divorced. Kee-Kee liked her instantly, and after we discussed it, Shelia kept her on the days I worked.

Ever since the advisor told me I wasn't smart enough, school became less interesting. There was a conflict between work and school hours. I couldn't do both, so I dropped out.

The luxurious retirement facility was tucked away in the suburbs of Marietta. Mrs. Gladys was dignified and sharp as a whip to be ninety years old. She spoke of her husband (a prominent doctor) often who had been deceased for many years. The only assistance she needed was getting in and out of the shower and with breakfast. She made sure I knew to cut up a half banana into four slices in her Banana Nut Crunch cereal and add two creams and one sugar to her coffee. Everything was going well. Mrs. Gladys loved having me there, my relationship with Shelia became stronger and I was saving money. Then one day I got a phone call. "You have a collect call from "Shawn King," an inmate at a Correctional Facility."

"Hey, Jo!"

"Shawn! What are you doing in there? What happened?"

"Armed robbery. I gotta do four years. I coulda got ten! I'm all right Jo, don't cry. It's a lot of my boys in here from Hartsville. They gon look out for me. I got a cool cellmate, he's from Columbia. I'll probably get out after two on good behavior and do the rest on probation."

The automated operator interrupted us. "You have one minute remaining."

"I need you to put some money on my books. Take my address and send me some pictures of you and Keetie-Weetie (his nickname for Kee-Kee) I Luv Ya!" Whenever a crisis hit, I panicked. It meant I had to stop everything I was doing and focus on Shawn. I was worried about him being in prison and not having anyone to rely on but me.

Crisis also triggered my sex drive. Sex was a coping mechanism and the only thing I felt I could control. I felt like Shawn was my responsibility. I felt guilty about not being able to protect him when we were little. He told me about the time when his fingers were frost bitten and he went to the hospital. He said he told them he was homeless, and they treated him and sent him back in the freezing cold without asking why. How adults in the medical field could do that to an eleven-year-old child is beyond me. I promised myself that day I would never turn my back on him. The money I was saving to find another place, I started using to send Shawn money for shoes, clothes, commissary and the daily collect calls that were astronomical. This is all Bert and Howard's fault for the situation Shawn was in. I delved deeper into what was causing my behavior and discovered that my actions were a direct result of my childhood trauma. Impulsivity, low self-esteem, co-dependency, manipulation, approval seeking, dysfunctional relationships, and the list goes on. After binging on sex with multiple men, I was ready for a change. Leon was always in my shadow, but he rotated between me and Bonnie.

Bonnie lived in North Carolina, and she and Leon were roommates and lovers long before I came into the picture. Leon was always upfront about their relationship, which continued even when she was married to someone else. Leon and I never discussed where we stood with each other. We just assumed we both knew what it was and didn't have to put a title on it but allowed it to develop into whatever it was supposed to be.

Leon had confessed his love for me, or at least his definition of love. What he didn't realize was he couldn't love me the way I needed to be loved. None of the men I'd been intimate with took the time to get to know me. Leon knew of me for a long time, but even he didn't know much about me. But he was extremely nice and someone I saw as a great friend but not a mate. There was so much more I wanted to see and do. Leon was routine and predictable, and he preferred to play it safe. I, on the other hand, lived by the seat of my pants.

Shawn was incarcerated at Lieber Correctional Institution in Ridgeville, South Carolina. I took the four-and-a-half-hour drive each way to see him once a month. We sat at the table in the visitation room surrounded by armed guards. We talked, laughed, played Pitty Pat card games, and ate tons of junk food from the vending machine. "My cellmate saw your picture and wanted me to ask you if he could write you."

"What does he look like?"

"I ain't judging no other man, Jo. Darren is cool. Smart as hell too." Shawn said, tapping his finger on his head. "Pitty Pat!"

"Well, he must not be too smart, he's in here. What is he in here for anyway?"

"Imma let him tell you that."

"He didn't kill anybody did he?"

"Nah, it ain't nothing like that."

"Okay, tell him to write me and send me a picture."

When I got the letter from Darren, I was impressed with his excellent penmanship and how well he wrote. And pleasantly surprised at how good looking he was: tall, slim, cute squinty eyes and a dazzling smile. He looked very reserved and studious. Darren didn't share in the letter what he was in for, but it had to be serious because Lieber was a maximum-security prison. Darren and I wrote each other every week. He just so happened to be nearby one day when I was on the phone with Shawn. "Yo, Darren! Somebody wanna speak to you."

"Hello?"

"Darren?" I asked.

"Yeah, this is Darren."

"This is Joretta. How are you?"

"I'm good now. I finally got a chance to talk to you. How are you?"

I thought I was going to pass out. Darren sounded even better than he looked. His voice was sexy, warm, melodic and smooth. Why did he have to be in prison? He had already reeled me in with the letters. After hearing his voice, I was captivated, and began accepting collect calls every day and sometimes twice a day. The night before my first visit with him was like Christmas Eve. I was so excited I barely slept. What if the picture he sent me is someone else?

It took about thirty minutes for him to come out. Our eyes locked as he walked toward me—both of us smiling from ear to ear. I stood up and fell into his arms. "Hey, baby." Darren was smiling from ear to ear. "You just don't know how long I've been waiting for this day to come," he whispered.

Darren embodied all the physical attributes of a Leo: huge nostrils, prominent cheekbones and broad shoulders. The monthly trips became twice a month. One visit for Shawn and the other one for Darren. He shared with me on the next visit his charge and sentence. I thought I was going to go into cardiac arrest. "Before I tell you what my charge and sentence is, I want you to know I didn't do all of what they charged me with. And I know that's what everybody says. I also understand if you don't want to communicate with me anymore after I tell you."

Can you please get to the point? I said to myself.

"I'm serving an 85-year sentence," Darren responded.

"Eighty-five years!?!?!?!" I guess I must have said it very loud because everyone in the visitation room looked at us. "How many people did you kill?"

Darren smiled and kept his composure. "I was charged with first-degree burglary for robbing a jewelry store after midnight. There was a string of burglaries during that time that were never solved so they charged me with all of them. They offered me a plea deal of 50 years. I turned it down, so the judge gave me 85." His voice was unsteady.

"Baby, I'm not going to do 85 years. I've been working on my case ever since I've been here and I will get out one day."

That's what everybody says too, I told myself.

"I just need you to believe that and wait for me." Darren was nineteen when he went in, he was now twenty-five. In eighty-five years, we'll both be dead. Call it love, naivete, or just plain stupid, but I was all in. Why wouldn't I be? Every man who showed up in my life I believed they were supposed to be there. I rationalized my relationship with Darren. Had Shawn not gone to that prison I would have never met him, so it had to have been predestined. I met his parents, brother and his four-year old son.

Deborah was one of the few people who knew about Darren. I was selective about who I shared it with. I knew most people wouldn't understand. Deborah was the kind of friend who never sugar-coated anything. She let me know how she felt about it. "Joretta, what in the hell are you going to do with a man in prison serving that kind of time?"

"He's going to get out one day, Deborah."

"Yeah, he sure will. In a box."

"Deborah don't say that. He told me he is going to get out and I believe him. I love him and he loves me."

"Well, if you say so. At least you'll always know where he is." Deborah started laughing.

"That's not funny, Deborah."

"You're a beautiful girl, Joretta, and I'd hate to see you waste your life on a jailbird. Especially when you don't know anything about him other than what he's told you." I knew Deborah meant well, but I had to go with my heart. And my heart said Darren was the one. Unlike all the other relationships where sex was the basis of the relationship, conversations were all Darren and I had. The prison didn't allow conjugal visits, so we had no choice but to talk. I was willing to prove Deborah and everybody else wrong. Darren and I proposed to each other. He submitted the paperwork to the prison and waited for their approval. Once everything cleared, we started making plans to get married at the prison chapel.

Around the eight-month mark, the excitement started to wear off. The wear and tear on my car, all-day visits and long-distance phone calls were taking a toll on me. The $300.00 monthly phone bills and putting money on the books for him and Shawn were draining me financially. Thanksgiving and Christmas when the prison allowed inmates to have outside food, Darren requested shrimp, crab cakes, seafood pasta and New York-style strawberry cheesecake.

He was friends with another inmate who was from Atlanta and suggested his girlfriend and I connect so we could carpool to prison. Debbie lived on the south side of town. She and Carl dated before he went to prison. I still had to drive my car to her house to pick her up, adding an additional hour to my drive. But she was sweet, and it was nice having the company and help with driving. When Shawn called me, he said Darren told him about our engagement. "I thought yall was just gon write each other, he talkin bout yall getting married. What in the hell you gon do wit somebody serving 85 years? I wouldn't even want no woman if I had to do that kind of time."

Shawn was always protective of me, even in prison. That was his way of telling me I was wasting my time. Deep in my heart, I knew the chances of Darren and I being together were slim to none, but I didn't want to let go of that feeling.

We were almost a year in, and I was still trying to hang in there. Reality started to set in along with the mental and emotional stress of forcing myself to prove that I could stick it out. Shawn was transferred to a minimum-security prison which meant two trips a month to two different prisons.

It was Sunday, March 8, 1992. "Hey, Jo." I could tell from Gail's somber tone something was wrong. "Howard died today." The tears that flowed steadily were for many reasons: sadness, anger and relief. I was genuinely sad about my daddy passing. I was angry that it wasn't Bert. I always said the day she died is the day I can start living. That's just how much animosity I had toward her. I was relieved because I didn't have to go back to Hartsville and see him suffering.

We all came together at Howard's funeral and dispersed as soon as it was over. It was sad and awkward being that it had been a long time since the family had seen or communicated with each other. It was especially difficult to see Shawn at the back of the chapel, shackled with a prison guard on each side. When I returned home, I wrote Darren a letter of apology that I could no longer be there for him and told him not to call or write me anymore. My one year in the projects was approaching. Most of my savings had dwindled. I used what was left to rent a townhouse and moved out of the projects.

CHAPTER 7

Sometimes your heart needs more time to accept what your mind already knows.

- Paulo Coelho

——— - Bleach on Colored Clothes - ———

Darren is probably heartbroken over my letter. I know he couldn't wait to open it. I now regretted the things I'd said. Telling him how much money I had wasted on him, that he was a liar and had probably done everything he was accused of, and he was never getting out of prison. If I had the courage to be honest with him about how I felt, I'm sure he would've understood.

After evaluating the relationship with Darren, as weird as it felt, it was my way of being in control and needed. It was a distraction from having to face those ugly thoughts and voices telling me I was ugly, stupid and unlovable. The first step to recovery in any addiction is admittance. I knew I had serious sexual and mental problems. I just didn't know what to fix or how to do it. The stigma associated with mental health in the Black community prevented me from speaking about it openly.

The astrological myth of being a Scorpio was my excuse for having a high sex drive. Having sex with multiple partners and enjoying it is one thing. Having sex with multiple partners who I found repulsive is another. Deborah would always tell me, "I don't know why you won't just marry Leon. You know he loves your dirty drawers." Leon was always there waiting patiently for me to realize he was the one. He was the nice guy I said I wanted but complained he was too nice. However, as nice as he was, he wasn't flawless.

My assignment with Mrs. Gladys was coming to an end soon. I'd obtained my certified nursing license and got a job at a nursing home working the third shift. I thought about what Deborah said about Leon and committed to a monogamous relationship. Working at the nursing home was exhausting. To make ends meet, I picked up a second job. Leon commuted from South Carolina to Georgia every weekend. He did what he could to help but it wasn't enough for me to quit one of my jobs. A missed period was never a good sign, especially when having unprotected sex and no longer on birth control.

With all the birth control available, you'd think I would be smart enough to prevent an unplanned pregnancy. I prayed it was stress from working two full-time jobs. Well, at least this time Leon and I are together. "Guess what? I'm pregnant."

"You pregnant?" Leon looked as disappointed as he sounded.

"Yeah, I'm pregnant."

"Well, now is not a good time." He told me.

"What are you suggesting?"

"Now Joretta, you already got Kee-Kee. You ain't in no position to take care of another one. I'm still living in Columbia and getting ready to go to truck driving school. I ain't got time for no lil crumb snatcher rat now. Maybe later when I get some years on the road, but not now. You need to have another abortion." The mention of the word abortion caused my body to tense up. I could feel the sharp, stabbing pain; the cold dark room sent chills throughout my body.

"I can hear my baby's cry from his body being pulled apart by the hands of a white man who didn't give a damn about him or his Black Mama! But his Black daddy paid him to do it!" And you want me to go through that again!" I told Leon.

"Now Joretta, it don't take all that. Hell, you talking bout having a baby. I ain't even got the money to pay for the abortion. Imma have to borrow the money. I sho as hell can't take care of no child rat now." It was obvious Leon had made up his mind and mine too about what I needed to do with my body. He borrowed the money from Jean, and she took me to get the abortion. At least this place put me to sleep. After the procedure was over, Jean took me back to her house to recover. I told Leon we needed to take a leave of absence from each other. My new obsession became food. I tried to eat away every pain, broken heart and disappointment I had gone through. The more weight I gained, the more unattractive and depressed I felt and the more abusive I became.

The older Kee-Kee got the more she resembled Bert. I wanted to get as far away from that lady as possible. Here she was staring me right in the face through the eyes of my daughter. No matter what Kee-Kee did, it wasn't good enough. I can't recall a time when she was disobedient or disrespectful. I never got a phone call from any of her teachers about her being disruptive. She did her homework every day after school and was always appreciative of everything I did for her. She never complained about the food she ate or the clothes she wore. Yet, I took all my anger and frustration out on her. I would cuss her out if I didn't like the way she sneezed.

Things that would be considered trivial to a sensible person, infuriated me. The rinse cycle on the washing machine started and I was looking for my downy ball to put the fabric softener in it. "Kee-Kee!!!! Have you seen my Downy ball?"

"No mom. I haven't seen it."

"You're telling a Goddamn lie! Get your ass down here now and find my damn Downy® ball!" Kee-Kee came downstairs crying and trembling. She held her head down afraid to come close to me knowing what was coming next if she didn't find it. I never apologized to Kee-Kee for beating her and accusing her of misplacing the Downy® ball after I found it in the dryer where I'd left it. I hated myself for the way I treated my child.

James was the assistant store manager. He came to work every day in a crisp white collared shirt and tie. His jacket draped across his left arm and flat cap in his right hand. "Hey sis, wait up!" I thought he was trying to stop me for something work-related.

He told me he had been watching me for a while and asked if I was married. He said he had just gotten out of a relationship and asked if he could take me out. He asked for my number and gave me his number and address. James was cordial, polite and charming. He called and left several voice messages, but I never returned his calls. The next time he saw me at work, he asked, "why didn't you return my calls? Give me your address, I'm coming to see you tonight when I get off work. Now, can I get a hug?"

I leaned in making sure not to get too close.

"Why are you giving me a church hug?" We both laughed. "I'll see you tonight."

The voice of reasoning was saying one thing and my body was saying another. I was very much attracted to him, and his persistence turned me on. I told myself I wasn't going to invite him in. We were just going to sit outside and talk. If that's the case, why am I cleaning up like crazy, showering, shaving and splashing on Vanilla Fields perfume? Maybe he won't show up.

I heard a knock at the door. There he was, gleaming like the moon and radiating like the stars. Forget what I said earlier about not inviting him in. I don't know if I was more stunned by the jet-black silky-smooth hair covering his huge muscular chest or his huge biceps that were proudly branded with the Kappa Alpha Psi symbol. Aside from his good looks and great build, he was smart, sexy and witty.

Twenty-four hours later, I was thinking about how nice Joretta Johnson sounded. It was the simple things: sweet messages and songs he left on my voicemail, the corny jokes he told, and the times he played air guitar butt naked, that had me all giddy and goo-goo over him. Like a spider catching its prey, James had trapped and spun me into his web.

My head was so far in the clouds, it didn't matter that it had been five months, and James hadn't taken me on the date he requested. Nor did it matter that I never went to his house. He always came to mine but never spent the night. Well, we both worked a lot. It was easy to make excuses than to listen to what my gut was telling me. James is either married or has a girlfriend. Only time will tell.

I was a little reluctant to answer the questions on the questionnaire: "how many full-term pregnancies, abortions and miscarriages have you had?" I sat in a corner waiting for my number to be called. My eyes scanned the waiting room secretly judging the teenage girls and young women as to whether they were there for pregnancy tests, STD tests or W.I.C. food vouchers (women, infant and children), thinking I was different because I had a job and my own place. But when you're asking for government assistance, you quickly find out just how insignificant you are.

"Your pregnancy test came back positive." I wished my tears were tears of joy. "Is the father around?" I was offended the nurse asked that question, and that she assumed he wasn't. The nurse was an older Black woman whom I'm sure had seen her share of young single Black females with the same story. I told her that James was around for now, but I didn't know what his reaction was going to be when I told him. "You're a beautiful young lady. You've got to know your worth and love yourself before you can love anyone else."

Regardless of how James reacted to the news, having an abortion was not an option. "I'm pregnant."

"Okay. What do you want to do? Have an abortion? Have the baby and give it up for adoption?" James spoke with great candor and honesty. I was relieved to know I would not have to go through this pregnancy alone. James was so caring and attentive. He wanted to know about my doctor visits and how I was feeling. He suggested we start shopping for baby items. Shortly thereafter the calls ceased. He wasn't coming by anymore and I didn't see him at work, but I wanted to give him the benefit of the doubt. A couple of weeks later James reappeared. He said he had a family emergency out of town and had to leave on a moment's notice. He reassured me he would be there for me, and I wanted to believe him.

It was Friday night, James called and said he needed to borrow my car to go to work. "Come to the house and pick me up and I'll take you back home." It was a modest townhouse with a patch of grass and weeds. James got in the car and took me back home. "I'll bring your car back in the morning when I get off work and you can take me home."

Saturday morning came. No James, no car. Maybe he was tired after he got off and went home to take a nap and will bring my car later. I was working a part-time job at the cable company on the weekends. Luckily it was a few miles from my house and the cab fare was only a few dollars.

My coworkers Paige and Tanya worked on the weekends and the three of us became very close friends. On Sunday I still hadn't heard from James and had to take a cab to work again. When Paige noticed my car wasn't outside, she asked, "Joretta, where's your car?"

"James took my car Friday and I haven't heard from him since."

"What do you mean he took your car? Have you called him?" I told her I did, but I didn't tell her there was a woman's voice on the voicemail. "Pick up the phone and call him now!" Paige was assertive and direct. Like a child being ordered by a parent, I picked up the office phone and slowly dialed James's number, hoping no one would answer.

"Hello?" the female voice said. "May I speak to James?' I could barely get the words out. My palms were sweaty and my heart was racing, and Paige was sitting at her desk directly across from me making facial expressions.

"Who is this?" The voice asked me.

"This is Joretta."

"Joretta, James is sleeping. What can I do for you?"

I covered the phone with my hand and whispered to Paige, "It's a lady on the phone, she said James is asleep."

"Well ask who in the hell is she?" Paige said.

"Who am I speaking to?" I asked her.

"Victoria, I'm his wife." It felt like my heart stopped and all the blood had drained from my body, and I was going to collapse. I whispered to Paige what she had said.

"Give me the damn phone!" Paige held out her hand.

I knew what would happen if Paige had gotten on the phone. I told Victoria that I was six months pregnant from James and he had my car. "I have your car and I'm getting ready to drive it to work." she replied.

She never acknowledged what I said about being pregnant. I told Paige what she said. "Let's go get your damn car!" Paige was furious. She took me to James's house and my car wasn't there. He came outside and his wife stood in the doorway laughing and said she hid my car. I called the police. When they arrived, they told James if he didn't find it, he would be arrested. We eventually found my car in an adjacent parking lot.

I was absolutely devastated and enraged that I allowed this to happen. The signs, red flags and caution lights were there. I chose to ignore them because my feelings were tangled in the web that James had weaved, and I couldn't see the forest for the trees. The endless laughter and sweet voicemails seemed so genuine. Why did he have to lie?

I sank to such a low level of depression, my doctor suggested I speak to a therapist. I didn't need a therapist, I needed revenge. I contemplated how I could make him pay for what he'd done. I subscribed to every magazine, ordered pizzas from every restaurant I could, and called every taxi company and sent them to his address. When my thoughts shifted from harassment to homicide, I knew it was time to seek professional help. I was reluctant to see a psychiatrist because of my last encounter with the one in Hartsville.

My appointment was with a Black female psychiatrist. On the first visit I did all the talking while she took notes. After several visits, she diagnosed me with borderline personality disorder and prescribed Prozac. "So, you're saying I'm crazy? I'm not crazy. Hurt, but not crazy."

"Ms. King, this doesn't mean you're crazy. You just need something to regulate your emotions. Let's see how you do with the medication and weekly visits and perhaps at some point we can wean you off the medication." Dr. Cannon also recommended books on psychological disorders and Adult Children of Alcoholics.

While Prozac helped with my depression and unwanted urges, I was anxious and nervous about bringing a baby into a toxic situation. I thought about what Deborah said about Leon being a good man. So, I called him and told him we needed to make our relationship exclusive. For whatever reason Leon chose to tell his family I was pregnant with his baby. When I found out they were on their way to Georgia bearing gifts to celebrate Leon's first-born son, I was beyond humiliated. I could've played along being that James wasn't going to be involved, but I couldn't. I told him he needed to tell them the truth. It was bad enough the first time meeting his mother was when he cheated on his girlfriend, now the second time is her thinking I cheated on him, got pregnant and didn't know who the father was. I cussed him out and told him how stupid he was for saying that and told him I didn't want to see him anymore.

I gave birth in March to a beautiful baby boy (I named Jameal) who was a carbon copy of James. Tanya and Gail were in the delivery room with me and took pictures of the birth. I sent them to James so he would know how to contact me if he wanted to see his son. I had gained an excessive amount of weight and made the decision to stop taking the medication. Jameal's nonstop crying and my postpartum depression caused me to have a mental breakdown to the point where I took him back to the hospital and told them they could have him back.

The doctors and nurses told me to leave him there for a couple of hours and go for a drive and come back to get him. I returned after an hour and he was sound asleep. They told me anytime I needed a break to bring him by. Every time the phone rang, I'd hope it was James. When Jameal turned three months, I finally got the call from James saying he wanted to see his son and I wanted to see James too.

One look into his big, beautiful eyes and the warmth of his wide smile was all it took. I had forgotten about everything I had called him. He reminded me how good of a lover he was. Everyone deserves a second chance. He asked me for pictures of Jameal to show his mother and asked what I needed. I gave him a list and he said he would be back the following day. I guess he got his days mixed up because the following day never came.

I'd ascertained that James's visit wasn't about seeing his son. It was a ploy to dissuade me from filing child support. We never discussed it but I'm sure he'd thought about whether I would pursue it or not. And he was right. I had already contacted the Georgia Department of Child Support Services (DCSS) and was told I had to wait until Jameal turned a year old before I could file. Like always, I found my solace in food. Tanya, Paige and I would meet up with our children once a week at the Old Country Buffet or Ryan's Steakhouse and ravage the buffet. If it weren't for them, I don't know what I would've done. They were always there when I needed to cry, vent and let out my frustration.

The weekly trips to the buffet and dinner at Outback Steakhouse® finally caught up with me. Going from a size 12 to a 16 was my breaking point. It was after midnight; I was in the bed eating Oreo cookies and a half gallon of Neapolitan ice cream.

There was a super fit petite woman prancing around on-stage in spandex and a sports bra shouting "Stop the Insanity!" She was telling her story of how she was obese and depressed and what she did to lose the weight. Her before and after pictures were incredible. What she said was very simple: move your body and eat healthy. She talked about how she cut out all the bad foods and started eating better and walking.

I couldn't believe it was the same person. I thought if she could do it, so could I. Right then and there I threw the ice cream and cookies in the trash and threw away all the junk food in the cabinets and refrigerator. One by one I eliminated meat, starting with pork, beef, turkey, chicken and finally fish. I adopted a vegan diet. Ironically, Indian food became one of my favorite foods because of the flavors and spices. I thought about how I didn't appreciate it at the time when I visited the little girl in North Carolina. I started walking every day and eventually started feeling better and looking better.

I kept a low profile for the most part and avoided seeing people as much as I could. Within a year, I was a brand-new person physically, spiritually and mentally. I felt so good about myself. The cable company promoted me to supervisor. I paid my car and credit cards off. I had stellar credit, a nice savings, and I was going to start the process of buying a home. I'd read the books Dr. Cannon recommended and anything else I could find to help me heal.

One book was *To Thine Own Self Be True* by Cort R. Flint. He talked about temptation and wrote:

When an evil spirit goes out of a man, it travels over dry country looking for a place to rest; if it doesn't find one, it says to itself, "I will go back to the house which I left." So, it goes back and finds the house clean, and all fixed up. Then it goes out and brings seven other spirits even worse than itself, and they come and live with it. So that man is in worse shape when it is all over than he was at the beginning.

I highlighted and read that passage over and over, understanding that I was going to be faced with many temptations. I was close to celebrating a year of celibacy and vegetarianism, and I was in great shape. The day after Jameal's first birthday I hired an attorney to file child support, and James was ordered to pay $500.00 a month. This time his flattery didn't work. Forgiveness was a huge part of my healing, so I wrote a list of people whom I had to forgive and ask to be forgiven. Bert was at the top. I went to Hartsville where she was living with Mr. Billy in an upstairs dilapidated apartment. She looked like she'd aged thirty years since I last saw her.

But if I were going to get any answers from her, it had to be now because from the look of things, time was not on her side. "Bert, can I ask you a few questions?" She looked up at me and dropped her head back down. "Why didn't you take care of me and Shawn?"

"Girl, what in da hell you talkin bout? Ain't nobody wanna hear that shit you saying. You talking loud and saying nothing." The sick feeling in my stomach let me know this was a bad idea. I went back to Atlanta feeling worse than I did before, but at least I tried. Leon was the second person I had to forgive. We talked and he refused to admit he'd done anything wrong. He believed just because abortion was legal, it was right. "I wouldn't mind having a lil crumb snatcher now that I'm driving a truck. I would like to be married first." Leon never asked me to marry him, but I interpreted it as an indirect proposal.

So, I said, "Let's get married."

"Okay." We found a wedding chapel a couple of hours away. The time it took to drive to the courthouse, apply and receive the license, the inner voice and caution signs were flashing, telling me not to do it. The night before I was warned not to go through with it, but I thought it was cold feet. There was a battle between my mind and spirit.

The mind: Aren't you tired of paying all these bills and taking care of these children by yourself?

The spirit: You're independent. You can take care of yourself, and you don't need to depend on a man. Plus, you know you're not in love with him.

The mind: What's Love Got to Do with It? You can learn to love him.

The Spirit: Don't do it. At least not now, not like this. Take some time to think it over.

I told Leon the night before we needed to wait and that I felt like we were rushing into it. I told him I had already started the process of buying a house and it was something I wanted to have for my children. Leon may have been a little obtuse, but he was cynical. He saw this as his chance to entrap me and used everything he could think of to convince me that it would be almost impossible to take care of myself and he succeeded. We got married the next day on my birthday.

CHAPTER 8

For those choosing to break generational cycles, your parents couldn't do it. Their parents couldn't do it. But for some reason, you noticed the pattern and decided it ends with you. You're the prototype. So much power you have.

- Louisa May Alcott

—————— - Bleach on Colored Clothes - ——————

There were mixed reactions when I shared the news that Leon and I had eloped. Some thought it was a joke while others gave me their blessings. I allowed those who expressed their disapproval to influence my judgment. So, I contacted a lawyer to get the marriage annulled. To my dismay, the state of Georgia didn't grant annulments. Before filing for a divorce, I had to stay married for a year. A lot can happen in a year. We bought a brand-new house, furniture and a new car. I occupied myself with acquiring things, because the more I looked the part, I would feel the part. I wanted to be like the neighbors, picture-perfect: two parents, two children and a dog. But the more things I accumulated, the more I wanted, and the more miserable I became. I felt stifled, trapped and angry that I had given up my independence.

I relied on Leon to pay a mortgage I couldn't afford even though I was the primary borrower. I went from being debt free to having seven maxed-out credit cards and a depleted savings account. I had dug a hole too deep to climb out of. I accepted defeat and decided to give Leon and marriage a chance. I never had to pay the mortgage, car payment, insurance, utilities or buy food. He was a good man and a great provider, but there was still something missing.

I checked the calendar and made sure to have sex during ovulation. When I told Leon I was pregnant, his response was, "oh yeah?" Now that we're married there's no excuse not to have a baby. We decided we would wait until after the second trimester to share the news. Terry had reached out to me and told me Ashley wanted to see me. She was twelve years old when she came to visit. It was awkward, to say the least.

I spent most of my time apologizing and taking her shopping. I presented to Ashley a patient, loving mother. Kee-Kee watched my every move and knew I was being disingenuous. However, it was the first time I felt like I was doing something right.

Eight weeks into my pregnancy I started having unbearable stomach cramps. I figured it was exhaustion from all the running around. But the pain intensified, and I started spotting. By the time I got to the E.R. I had already miscarried. Leon was on the road when I told him the news, "Well, thangs happen." That was all he had to say about the death of his third child. That is his third child with me. He told me there were three other women pregnant from him prior to meeting me and they all had abortions. It was clear to me at that moment that Leon didn't want any children. It was also at that moment I contemplated my exit. I'd work, pay off my debts, save some money and leave once Kee-Kee graduated from high school and went off to college.

Everything I had planned started to fall apart. I was fired for taking a two-hour lunch and found out Kee-Kee was pregnant after getting a letter in the mail from Planned Parenthood®.

I was livid! It angered me even more to learn the father was a white boy. I was told that white men were taught they weren't a man until they had sex with a "wench[4]." I drove to Kee-Kee's school and checked her out. She knew from the look on my face my reason for being there was not good.

---

[4] The history of the word wench is ugly and sordid. Initially it was a medieval term that meant a single woman that later evolved to be synonymous with a prostitute. During the period in U.S. history when Black people were enslaved, it was applied to Black women who were forced to be concubines to their white slave master. Post abolition, it came to be a racial slur given to Black women who had relationships with white men, believed to be doing so for the sole purpose of raising their status in society.

"So, you wanna tell me what you're going to do about your baby?" Kee-Kee looked terror-stricken and started crying.

"I'm sorry, mom."

I screamed, yelled and called her every bitch and whore I could think of. "How dare you get pregnant when you know what I've been through? What are you going to do about college? You're going to have an abortion."

Kee-Kee looked at me and said, "I'm keeping my baby and as far as college, who's to say I was going to college even if I didn't get pregnant." She knew this was the only time she could talk back to me and not get the breath knocked out of her.

"Okay, you wanna be grown. I tell you what. You won't be bringing that mutt[5] in my house. You need to get out!" I wasn't going to kick Kee-Kee out on the streets pregnant. I found a home for pregnant teenagers, submitted the paperwork, and she was accepted. It was a beautiful mansion in an inconspicuous neighborhood in Buckhead. Kee-Kee was scheduled to report the following week. I waited for her to get home from school so I could take her.

Hours went by and she didn't come home. I found out the next day she had moved in with her boyfriend and his parents. That same year Ashley got pregnant and was having issues with Terry and had to come live with me.

"Hey, Jo." I immediately recognized the voice on the other line. "It's your brother Smoky. I'm in Atlanta. Come pick me up." The area he said he was in was not good. I didn't want to drive there, plus I was still somewhat afraid of him. I told him I would come and get him knowing I wasn't. Smoky was known for missing in action but would always reappear. About a month later we received a call that he had been in the morgue. He had jumped from the overpass in downtown Atlanta.

For a long time, I blamed myself for not going to pick him up. I didn't want Ashley to move in after making Kee-Kee leave but I did it to earn her love. Leon constantly reminded that he paid all the bills and that without him I couldn't survive. He was partially right. I was somewhat complacent.

---

[5] Although commonly used to refer to mixed breed dogs, with respect to humans, mutt is a derogatory term that dates back to the 19th century, used to describe people of more than one race. It is synonymous with the terms mongrel and mulatto (the latter of which is controversial as many Biracial and mixed-race people of today have come to use it to self-identify). In general, it is not used as a compliment when one person says it about another person.

I had no real marketable skills. Customer Service was the only thing I'd done, and it barely paid above minimum wage.

What more could I do? I rekindled my relationship with food. I stayed home all day and stuffed myself with every carb I could find and drank a big glass of Epsom salt water immediately after to eliminate in hopes of not gaining weight.

Months went by I still didn't have a job. I was depressed and discouraged. I got a call from the teacher that Jameal was under the table in the cafeteria looking under little girls' dresses. I would've passed it off as him being a curious five-year-old boy until she insinuated, he was a pervert. I didn't have enough confidence at the time to defend my son against a white teacher's allegations.

When Jameal came home, I took it out on him and slapped him so hard I left my handprint on his face. The next morning my handprint was still there. I sent him to school anyway thinking no one would pay it any attention. But the same teacher who accused my little black boy of being a Peeping Tom, reported it to DFACS (Department of Family and Children Services). A Black female social worker came to my house to investigate. She walked in and complimented me on how nice my home was.

She asked a few questions and said, "I know how hard it is raising Black children and you're under a lot of stress. We as Black people beat our children, but you can't leave marks on them. I'm going to close your case. Have a good day." I wasn't sure if I should've been thankful or disappointed that this lady from the agency who was supposed to protect children from abuse had just given me permission and instructions on how to abuse my child. If only she had known that was a huge mistake.

Every time I abused Jameal, I delivered body shots and forced him to sit in hot water when he took a bath. There was a weird feeling of power and pleasure I got out of abusing him. When Ashely gave birth to her son, I told her she had to go back to South Carolina. She didn't want to go and told me Leon had given her permission to stay as long as she wanted. We got into a heated argument that escalated into a physical fight.

The police were called and saw that we both had marks. He refused to press charges against us and told Ashley to leave. I tried my hardest not to be like Bert, but I exhibited her behavior in everything I did. I could relate to what it must have been like for her to get to the point where she was tired and just didn't want to be a mother anymore. I had reached that point. I was tired of being in a marriage where I felt like I had to prostitute myself for room and board because of the constant reminder that he was the breadwinner. I realized then that when you don't have any money people make decisions for you. When you make your own money, you make your own decisions.

I knew Leon loved me in his own way, but I wanted someone to be my friend and really get to know me and not just my vagina. Leon's love was just an emotional attachment to me. Too much damage had been done and the best thing he could do was to get out of the way.

I prayed and asked for forgiveness and direction. The next day something beautiful happened. I felt a calmness, peace and freedom I had never felt before. I cut off all my hair and got my nose pierced. I discovered Hatha Yoga and started eating healthy again. On our one-year anniversary, I filed for divorce, sold the house, and moved back into an apartment. The money Leon and I split from the sale of the house was enough to live off for six months giving me a little bit of time to look for a job. I saw an ad in the paper for a part-time seasonal receptionist at a day spa in Alpharetta, GA. I got the job, and from the first day I knew that was where I was supposed to be. Within a year, I went from part-time to full-time and promoted to supervisor.

Things finally seemed to be turning around. A couple of coworkers invited me out. A handsome man came to our table and offered to buy us drinks. I told him, "I'll have a cranberry juice and sprite." He came to the table several times throughout the night to check on us. As we started to leave, he asked if he could walk me to my car. *Just let him walk you to your car and do not give him your number*, the voice said. I honestly tried to ignore the little voice, but I couldn't resist his sweet smile and gave him my number. *You've been warned*, whispered the voice.

CHAPTER 9

Too often we underestimate the power of a touch, a smile, a kind word, a listening ear, an honest compliment, or the smallest act of caring, all of which have the potential to turn a life around.

- Leo Buscaglia

- Bleach on Colored Clothes -

Michael called and asked me out. We met at a club and went straight to the dance floor. "What you know about house music?" he asked.

"I love house music! What do you know about it?"

"I'm from Chi-Town where house music originated," he said while showing off his fancy footwork. An hour later we were still on the floor bouncing and spinning around dripping in sweat.

"Okay, I need to take a break," I told Michael. We found a place in the corner and Michael went to get water. We were grooving to the music when suddenly, I felt a soft bite right on the carotid artery causing me to jump up. The sensation traveled down my spine to my lower back. Michael started laughing, "What's wrong?"

"Please don't do that!" I told him, knowing I wanted him to do it again and again, and he knew it too. I sat back down and Michael turned my head toward him; his lips were soft and warm. My body quivered as he slid his tongue inside my mouth. "Come on, let's get out of here," he said. I got in his car. We forgot all about where we were and made love right there in the parking lot.

Michael and I gelled so well. Every time we were together our conversation flowed. He was good looking, and his body was even better. He introduced me to his mother, and I could tell they weren't that close. She was aloof and had a dry personality. He shared with me that he hated his mother for physically and verbally abusing him as a child. He said she favored his younger sister and brother, whom she had from a white man she had since divorced. I was all too familiar with his story. There's a saying a man will treat his woman according to the relationship he has with his mother.

Our lovemaking was explosive! I couldn't imagine it getting any better or more interesting. However, Michael had other desires, fantasies and fetishes. I had never met anyone who was into phone sex before meeting him. When we weren't together, he had to have phone sex before going to bed. Some nights we'd go from sundown to sunrise and that still wouldn't be enough. He called me on my way to work and I would have to pull over and have phone sex with him. Throughout the day while I was at work, he called wanting phone sex and I'd have to find a secluded area.

My cell phone bills exceeded $400 a month from having phone sex. But I was just as addicted as he was. I was also madly in love with him and was willing to do just about anything to please him. On New Year's Eve, he invited me to a party at a hotel. It seemed like a typical party. As we made our way through the crowd, I noticed two topless women. One was sucking the other one's breasts. *Maybe they're drunk*, I said to myself. The deeper we got into the party, the weirder it got.

One couple came up to me and said a group of people were going up to their room to have an orgy and wanted to know if Michael and I wanted to join them. "Hell no!" I told him. An older Black man told me his wife was attracted to me and invited me to have a threesome. "No thank you, sir." None of the things I found to be strange, fazed Michael at all. "Michael, you wouldn't believe what this man just asked me."

"Chill out," he said.

"What's going on in here? Who are these people?"

"These are lawyers, doctors, judges, politicians, etc. People just like me and you who are having a good time. They are swingers." That was my first time ever hearing the term or knowing anyone who was into this lifestyle.

I had done some freaky stuff in my lifetime, but they had taken freaky to a whole other level. We had gone to the movies before, so I had no reason to suspect anything differently when we went to this theatre. It was during the day and there weren't many people there. We sat down and waited for the movie to start.

A white man sat behind me and asked if he could eat my pussy. "What the fuck did you just ask me?" Again, Michael sat calmly as if this was normal. I looked around and saw that's what everyone else was doing. Sucking dicks and eating pussy right in the middle of the theatre. Like the swingers' party, this was another place where the freaks met up.

No matter how kinky, freaky, pleasurable and painful our sex was, it wasn't enough to please him. Michael had a sexual appetite I don't think any woman could satisfy. I accepted his sexual escapades with other women and was hoping this was a phase Michael was going through and we could move on to a healthy, committed, monogamous relationship. When Michael was fired for having phone sex with a customer, I realized he was more than a sex addict; he had a serious illness that no amount of sex I gave him was going to cure.

Moving on from Michael was extremely difficult. I had given him so much of myself, my time and money. Money, I didn't have, but stellar credit to borrow ten thousand dollars so he could buy a car. They say time heals all wounds. It took a year for me to get to a point where it didn't hurt anymore. During that year I went to Aesthetics School and got my Aesthetician license. Unfortunately, by the time I had the opportunity to use it, 9/11 happened. The money I had was gone, and I living was living off credit cards and temporary work.

I wanted to expand my knowledge in the skincare industry and figured Colon Hydrotherapy would be a great adjunct to facials. I called around to see how much the course was and spoke to a lady who had her own practice and offered me an apprenticeship. Mary had been in the business for over twenty years and had a huge clientele. One of her clients was an older white man named Clark who came every week for a colonic. He was very comfortable with my being in the room.

Mary instructed me to massage Clark's arms and legs while she administered the colonic. After his session, he pulled me to the side and asked if I did massages. I told him I knew how to do a massage, but I wasn't licensed. He said it didn't matter and we exchanged numbers. It was after five o'clock in the afternoon on a Saturday when Clark called and asked if I could come over. We met at a Chevron station, and I followed him to his house, which was just a few blocks away. I had reservations the whole time, but I needed the money.

The only thing I knew about him was his name and number. We entered his house through the garage. The house was quiet, and a faint herbal scent of rosemary filled the kitchen.

When Clark took me to the basement is when I started having heart palpitations. All sorts of thoughts were running through my head. *What if he's a serial killer and he chops me up and puts me in the freezer?* When I reached the bottom of the stairs, there were whips, chains, leather straps, paddles and all kinds of sadism and masochism paraphernalia.

I'm not making it out alive, I said to myself. In the middle of the room was a massage table. "Come on over. I don't bite," he said. I tried to remain calm, but I was deathly afraid. Clark was a small man, no taller than 5'6". He had a beautiful olive skin tone, a gorgeous smile, big beautiful dark brown eyes and thick eyelashes, and he was in great shape for a man in his late sixties. Once Clark stripped naked and got on the massage table, my fear subsided.

He handed me a bottle of oil and I started massaging his shoulders and arms. When I started massaging his legs, he flinched, but I wasn't doing anything intentionally to turn him on. He told me I had a good touch and that was the reason why he asked for a massage.

I could tell by Clark's body response a massage wasn't all he wanted. I didn't care if he did want more, a massage was all he was getting. As soon as my hands touched his ass, I heard a gentle moan. Before I knew it, my hand had involuntarily slapped his ass. He flinched and let out a louder moan. The harder I slapped him, the more it turned him on and the louder he got. Clark asked me to spank him with the paddle. "I can't hit you with that. It's going to hurt."

I was confused as to why he wanted me to do that. Clark sat up, looked at me and smiled. "You can end the massage now." He got dressed and we went upstairs to the kitchen.

He handed me a check for $300.00. I had never made that much money in such a short period of time for doing so little work. I hadn't even finished the massage. "Have you ever heard of Dominatrix?" he asked. I shook my head no. "I want you to look it up when you get home," he said. The information I saw online was both disturbing and intriguing. The images were of white women dressed in leather garments with whips. The definition given was one who takes control in a sexual or non-sexual setting, inflicting pain on their submissive participant. I tried practicing what I'd read the next time I saw him, but it felt weird. Why would anyone want to feel pain? He kept asking me what I wanted him to do. I didn't know what to say.

I played it safe and spanked him with the leather belt. Clark taught me more than I learned online. He coached me on what to say, what he wanted, how he wanted it and the words to use.

It wasn't long before I became a master at humiliating him. Clark told me, "Joretta, you have no idea how much power you have." Perhaps he was right. I had allowed every man to make me feel as if I needed them. This was unlike any relationship I had been in. We were both fulfilling each other's needs. I needed to feel in control and Clark needed to be controlled.

Clark explained to me his reason for wanting to be humiliated. He was a land developer and built dialysis centers and million-dollar ranch condominiums in Georgia and several other states. He said all day long he told people what to do, so he wanted someone to make him feel powerless. The more I humiliated Clark the more he wanted.

I didn't understand what Clark got out of wanting to be beaten to submission, but I got the satisfaction of being able to take out my frustration on him and beat him for every molestation, rape, abuse, pain and broken heart I had gone through. It felt almost too good to be true that I was getting paid to beat a man and a white man at that. Clark explained in a letter he wrote to me about how thrilled he was. He wrote:

I need your word that all of this is kept a secret that I am, and have been, your white cock slave. I now know that when you humiliate me and make me beg while I am naked on my hands and knees, that you feel so powerful, that you control me and have made me your dirty little white slut. It makes me feel worthwhile and I get so hot when you make me submissive, and I know that you are going to beat my sorry white ass. When you completely control me and

make me beg and look at me down there naked on my hands and knees, I think
how pathetic and disgusting I am to be so under your control, knowing that
you are the only Black woman in the world who knows my secret. I am the
successful white man that grovels at the feet of my Black Mistress and licks her
feet to show you how much I crave what you have made me.

Our relationship reminded me of something I'd read in the book *The*
Body Keeps the Score: Brain, Mind, and Body in the Healing of Trauma by
Bessel A. van der Kolk. *The challenge of recovery is to reestablish ownership*
of your body and your mind—of yourself. This means feeling free to know
what you know and to feel what you feel without becoming overwhelmed,
enraged, ashamed or collapsed.

Clark requested to see me two to three times a week. If he couldn't see
me, we had phone sessions and I verbally abused him. Sometimes the
conversation only lasted ten minutes. Clark paid me generously for my
services. As our relationship progressed, I got to know him on a personal
level. He told me his parents came to America in the 1940s from Greece.

His father was a great cook and opened a small restaurant and later became
successful buying real estate. Clark majored in architecture and followed in
his father's footsteps. As successful as Clark was, I was surprised he never
married or had children. He said he had dated several women who wanted
to get married, but he wasn't ready.

His current relationship was with a woman who started out as his
housekeeper. He said he had literally taken her from the trailer park and
moved her to Ansley Park, one of Atlanta's most affluent neighborhoods.
Sharon was an attractive lady, 15 years younger than Clark. She was a self-
employed housekeeper. Clark introduced me to Sharon, and a few family
members as someone who assisted his housekeeper to dispel any suspicions
they may have had, and I played along.

His family thought I was the cat's meow. Sharon made sure to let me know
how well-kept she was. She bragged about the lavish lifestyle he provided for
her. Her million-dollar condo, the Mercedes Benz truck he paid cash for,
jewelry from Tiffany's, the first-class flights to Paris, and the $25,000 he
paid to have her cat's sex changed from a female to a male because it kept
getting urinary tract infections.

If she was trying to make me jealous it worked. I thought the $3000 to

$5000 checks I was getting was something, but I was being lowballed like a Mutha-Fucka! But I understood my assignment.

I should get him to have sex with me, get pregnant so I'll have income for life. But sex wasn't what Clark wanted from me, and we never had sex. He just wanted me to denigrate him. Clark did ask me what my long-term goal was. I told him I wanted to eventually have my own facial business and he told me to give him a start-up price.

I impulsively said $35,000. Clark had a lot of money, but he also gave away a lot of money. In addition to Sharon and myself, he was taking care of an elderly cousin, and he paid for Sharon and her daughter's plastic surgeries and her daughter to go to undergrad and graduate school. There were also ex-girlfriends who called constantly for money. One of them lived on his property in Forsyth County. As years went by, our friendship went far beyond anything I could ever imagine.

There were times when I visited Clark and sat at his kitchen table, drank tea, and listened to him talk about his Greek heritage, giving me a tour of his home and educating me on his expensive antique furniture designers, paintings and rugs, or reading one of his many history books from his massive library. Clark was a brilliant man and had a great sense of humor. The more I got to know him, the less I wanted to engage in S & M. Clark loved his father and spoke very highly of him. His face lit up when he talked about him. His mother on the hand was a different story. He said his mother told him she got pregnant with him immediately after marrying his father, but she wasn't ready to have children.

He said she hated him for that, and that he was an inconvenience. He said she was physically and verbally abusive. He said when he was thirteen, she would wait until he got in the shower and beat him with a leather belt for no reason and then laugh at him.

Clark buried his head in my lap and broke into tears. I consoled him and told him we didn't have to do S & M anymore. I had a revelation that day that despite Clark being a rich, educated, white man, his story and pain were the same as mine and others, *his mother*. In 2011 Clark made good on his word and gave me the money to open my facial business.

CHAPTER 10

Choosing is confusing. In some ways, we have a tendency to choose the wrong person or the wrong decisions in our life. It could lead us to a dead-end, left in darkness. Alone and clueless, just because it wasn't a right option from the very first place.

- Shaa Zainol

——————— - Bleach on Colored Clothes - ———————

One of the things I took away from knowing Clark was that I always had the power and a choice, and I no longer needed approval or validation from a man. I adopted a raw foods diet of fresh fruit, vegetables, nuts, seeds and grains. I discovered Kundalini Yoga and read books on creative visualization, Chakras, Tantra Sex and Reflexology. *Sexual Reflexology: Activating the Taoist Points of Love* by Mantak Chia and William U. Wei was another powerful book I discovered.

I knew from what little I had studied about reflexology there were reflex points on the bottom of the feet, the palms of the hands and ear lobes that corresponded with all our organs, but I wasn't aware of the reflex points in the sexual organs. The authors explained that the pituitary gland, lungs, nose and heart are all located on the head of the penis. The liver, eyes, small and large intestines, kidneys and gall bladder are located along the shaft.

Deep inside the vagina near the uterus are the heart and lungs. The authors stated, "Yet the most intense and powerful reflex points on the body are the sexual organs themselves…" They went on to say, "When the sexual organs of the male and female unite, a wonderful stimulation of energy is experienced through the whole body. Sexual intercourse is an ecstatic acupressure treatment. The Taoists call sexual intercourse "healing love" because of its deep healing properties."

I wanted to know every single function of my vagina. I educated myself on what the Skene's glands and the Bartholin glands were and where they were located. I learned about the three muscles in the vagina, one being Pubococcygeus, or PC muscle, which is also referred to as Kegel exercises to strengthen the vagina—the muscle Laura taught me to squeeze when I was ten years old. She just didn't know what it was called. I was introduced to the book, *Sacred Woman: A Guide to Healing the Feminine Body, Mine, and Spirit* by Queen Afua. In her book, she teaches how to honor and heal the womb.

She talked about the importance of loving our mate. She stated: "Women, be wise when you enter a Sacred Union, for when we make love with our man, we become all of whom and what he is. We women drink his essence into our womb, the entrance to our entire inner world. If he is troubled and in pain, or full of liquor or flesh or mind-altering substances, we become all of who he is through his sacred fluids."

I studied Tantra Sex, which focuses on breathing and sound techniques. The more I read, the more was revealed to me. Men trusted my alluring smile and revealed some of their darkest secrets. There was Roman, the nerdy Black coworker who was paid by white men to perform oral sex on him. (I got him fired a few weeks before his wedding for threatening me.) Then there was the 6'7" egotistical police officer with a baritone voice who had made his rounds with many women in Atlanta but found pleasure in getting his anus penetrated with an orange popsicle. There was also the white businessman who claimed to be racist but confided how he fantasized about having sex with Black women while making love to his white wife.

There was the successful white man who was a cokehead, obsessed with getting his anus penetrated with a Black dildo while he sniffed cocaine off another Black man's ass. I can't forget Wallace, a leader of a religious institution who practiced a strict vegan diet, but ate more pork and pussy than the law allowed. Then there was Mario who only wanted to lick yeast-infected vaginas. And all this time I thought I had issues. I had given men more credit than they deserved. The more I read, studied and meditated, the more my eyes were opened to men who on the outside portrayed confidence and high self-esteem to mask their insecurities, but deep down inside they were frightened little boys who had been damaged, physically, mentally and emotionally.

I transitioned from a raw foods diet to a fruitarian diet of nothing but fresh fruit. For six months I followed that diet to the letter, and it was the best I'd ever looked and felt. It gave me a calmness and peace I never knew existed. I used that time to go within and do some self-healing. It was the happiest time of my life. I was so ecstatic I forgot about what Cort R. Flint said in his book about the spirits leaving and coming back with seven other spirits. I thought I had enough discernment to recognize the wolves.

I was passing out some of my business cards in a shopping plaza. As I started to approach a car with some men sitting in it, I realized they were teenagers. "I'm sorry, I thought you all were older. I was going to give you some of my cards," I said. The young man in the passenger seat extended his hand for one.

"Okay, you can give it to your mother or sister." The next day I received a call from someone who said his name was Matthew and that I had given him my card. "Oh yeah, I remember. Do you want to schedule an appointment for your mother?" I asked.

He replied, "no, I was calling to holler at you."

I snickered and said, "Boy, how old are you?"

With all the confidence in the world, he said, "I'm eighteen and I've been with older women before."

"Boy, I have children older than you. Goodbye!" Matthew called again the next day. He asked me questions no man my age had ever asked. Simple things like, what was my favorite food, color, music, and if I liked sports. I didn't see any harm in talking to him. I told him I knew nothing about sports, but Jameal played baseball. He told me he played football and ran track. He said he would love to come to one of Jameal's games. Jameal had a game coming up that next weekend, which happened to be at a park close to where Matthew said he lived. I told him the time and he said he would be there. "Matthew? Where's your mother?" I asked.

"In jail," he said and hung up the phone. I had read a book called *A Still Small Voice* by Echo Bodine. I was very familiar with listening to the voice and aware of the consequences when you don't. I told myself Matthew could probably be a big brother to Jameal. And if his mother was really in jail, maybe there was a way I could help him. Matthew showed up to Jameal's game. He was a little rough around the edges, but I guess it was to be expected with his background.

He told me his mother had been in jail for a few months but was scheduled to be released in a couple of years. He said his sister and stepdad lived at home. I wasn't attracted to him and never looked at him sexually. After the game, we got something to eat, and he asked if he could come over to play the game with Jamel. Jameal seemed to like him, so I agreed. He stayed in Jameal's room and ate and played the game. When I told him it was time to leave and I was going to take him home, he said Jameal wanted him to spend the night. "No, that's not a good idea. I really don't know you and I'm sure your sister and stepdad will be worried about you." Jameal begged to let him stay and that was a BIG MISTAKE!

I had a two-bedroom condo, and the bedrooms were next to each other. I told him he could sleep downstairs on the sofa. Around 1 a.m., I got up to get a drink of water. I opened the fridge, turned around and Matthew was standing right in front of me. He grabbed me by the waist. *No!!! Not the carotid artery!* There were only two other men who had discovered that was one of my erogenous zones: Tony and Michael. I tried to refrain from being turned on, but my panting gave it away. He's too young, I told myself. I had been celibate for a while, and it was a real challenge because after six months of eating nothing but fresh fruits my sex drive had magnified!

I tried and tried and tried, but I eventually gave in. I knew this had to be the one and only time. The next day when I told him I was going to take him home he started wheezing like he was having an asthma attack. I panicked and asked him if he needed to go to the E.R. But what would I tell the paramedics? He's an 18-year-old boy who's been at my house all night who I really knew nothing about.

For all I know, he may not even be eighteen. What if he's underage? Luckily Jameal had an asthma inhaler, when I offered it to him, he said he was okay. I found out he faked the asthma attack so he wouldn't have to leave. My patience was getting thin, and I told him, "You need to leave and leave now. I'm going to take you home."

"Okay, you think you gon use me? I'll leave, but not before I go upstairs and tell your son I fucked the shit out of his mama last night!" Matthew proceeded to go upstairs; I begged him not to do that. I was able to get him to allow me to take him home by telling him I would see him again even though I had no intentions, but Matthew did. He showed up at my house the next day. When I didn't answer, he rang the doorbell constantly.

My condominium complex was small and quiet. Most people were professionals. My neighbor was a teacher. I was too embarrassed for her to see him, so I opened the door.

Matthew professed his love for me. I tried talking to him and telling him it was just a phase he was going through. He cried and told me he wanted to be with me for the rest of my life, even if he had to push me around in a wheelchair when I got old. It was bad. I felt so bad for him because I knew what it was like to feel that type of love. I knew it was my fault for allowing this to happen, but I didn't know what to do. I thought if I continued, it would eventually play out on its own.

I told Matthew he would meet a cute young girl his age and move on. I don't know how I thought continuing to have sex with him would help. I had used everything I'd learned about sex on him. After months of fighting, I gave in. In the beginning, the relationship was fun and cute. I felt like the teenager who never had a high school sweetheart had been freed.

I had missed out on that part of my life and Matthew had given it back even though I was 22 years his senior. My heart didn't see age. It only saw pure unadulterated love. I was called a child molester, predator and cougar by most. But Karen, Renay and Kam never passed judgment. Matthew, on the other hand, bragged to his friends, family and his football coach. He missed going to his prom because he said if I couldn't go, he wasn't going without me. He followed me everywhere I went, and if he even had an inkling another man was looking at me, he was quick to remind them I was his girl.

All these years I wanted a man to celebrate and appreciate me, and here was a boy telling me everything I wanted to hear and feel. But I wasn't stupid enough to think it could be anything long-term. Every time I tried to end it with Matthew, he became angry to the point where it started to scare me. It started with things I ignored like him taking my car without my permission and when I confronted him, he yelled at me and cussed me out.

Trying to shield Jameal from what was going on only empowered him to persist. If someone would have told me I would be a victim of domestic violence I would've laughed. However, I didn't consider the times Matthew refused to let me leave the house without him, his possessiveness, jealousy, name-calling, isolating me from family and friends, and cutting my hair were all signs of domestic abuse.

I should've known something was wrong with that boy when I picked him up from school and he came out of the special education trailer. And the time I sent him to the store to get some lemonade and he came back with a box of Capri Sun. I was embarrassed and ashamed to let anyone know because of his age. After all the hard work I had done to get where I was, I allowed an uneducated teenage boy to come into my life and bully me and my son. Matthew had taken total control over my life and manipulated my son. I saw Jameal change from a sweet little boy wearing Vans® and skateboarding to wanting to be a thug.

The times when I stood up to Matthew and told him to leave, I had to deal with him breaking the windows, breaking into my house, or making a scene in front of the neighbors. The police were called more times than I could count, they said because Matthew had been there for more than thirty days, he was considered a resident and he didn't have to leave but I could. As soon as the police left and I tried to leave, Matthew held me hostage and locked me in the room. I had to call Renay and have her call the police to come back out.

I now understood how Linda and so many women found themselves in abusive relationships, why they stayed and how dangerous it was to get out. I also understood the reconciliation. How they can be so apologetic, sympathetic and loving. It was that part of Matthew I loved and thought I could love his anger away, but like many abusers, he abused again.

During my annual exam, I found out I was four months pregnant. It was a complete and utter shock because I never missed a period and had no symptoms. Out of every attempt I tried previously to get Matthew to leave, getting pregnant was all it took. He was furious that I could still get pregnant at the age of forty-three and told me I needed to have an abortion because the baby would probably be born with special needs. There was no way I was going to have an abortion despite the circumstances. In March 2008 I gave birth to a healthy baby boy.

Matthew came around periodically and chose not to be active in his life. I lost so much due to that relationship, my condo, clients, money and time. But I also gained a lot. My baby who was so beautiful and precious and my friends who stood by me. It wasn't that Matthew was so much in love with me. He was in love with the feeling of someone caring about him because of the absence of his mother who wasn't there for him because she was dealing with her issues.

Like always, I started over and moved to a new place. I was exhausted. I had no more to give any man. The best thing for me to do was to stay by myself, because clearly I had done a terrible job with relationships. If men leave me alone, I'll leave them alone because I would never approach a man. Jameal had just turned thirteen and I could see a lot of Matthew in him, despite the fact they weren't related. When he got to high school, he started acting out. They said he had behavioral and anger issues. It triggered me, I cussed him out and waited until he got out of the shower and beat him naked with the belt buckle.

The school recommended professional counseling. He was able to get a Black male therapist who told me Jameal was traumatized from my abuse and the abuse he witnessed and heard that I wasn't aware of. The time Matthew slammed me against the wall and choked me. The nights sexual sounds echoed from my bedroom.

I thought if I wasn't around Bert, my life would get better. I thought by doing the opposite of what she did was all I had to do: work, take care of my children and not drink. Having to admit that I was repeating the cycle of abuse and behavior of Bert was hard to accept. It was also my belief that the most important part of being a good parent meant providing for my children financially. I was devoid of any emotional or psychological support.

I felt like a failure as a mom and thought they would have been better off without me. I wanted them to be proud of me, yet there wasn't anything I had done or accomplished for them to be proud of. I'd failed at every aspect of my life. Since relationships were what seemed to cause me the most grief, I avoided putting myself in any situation that could result in one. That nagging feeling, I had at the age of twelve of writing my book was very strong.

At the onset of writing my story, my fingers became extremely painful, and my hands swelled to the size of a grapefruit. After several visits to a rheumatologist and a series of tests, I was diagnosed with severe rheumatoid arthritis. All the time I spent eating healthy and exercising, I was devastated this was happening. Then I remembered reading something Dale Carnegie mentioned in his book about rheumatoid arthritis. Carnegie stated that Dr. Russell L. Cecil, a world-renowned authority on arthritis, listed long-cherished resentments as one of the four commonest conditions that bring on arthritis.

Whether or not that was my case, there was some truth to it. I had been harboring the wounds from my past all these years, I wouldn't doubt it contributed to it. I paused on my book and took a deeper look within to find the answers. I was told I needed to talk to Bert. But I didn't want to. I had already tried and it didn't work. Maybe she'll die soon, and I won't have to worry about it. I enrolled in online classes to get my degree in English. I was doing well in my classes. My facial business had picked up, I was saving money again, my health was improving and things were turning around.

CHAPTER 11

Not everything that is faced can be changed, but nothing can be changed unless it is faced.

- James Baldwin

─────── - Bleach on Colored Clothes - ───────

Call me stupid and a fool, but I was minding my business when Kelvin sent me a Facebook friend request. I hadn't seen him since we were teenagers, and I thought he was the cutest and smartest boy in the world. He had grown into a handsome man but still had the same bashful smile. He seemed to have done well for himself and appeared to be happy with his wife and two adult daughters.

He sent a private message thanking me for accepting his request. Days later, another message telling me how beautiful I was. We continued back and forth with playful flirty messages for a while, then transitioned to phone calls. Kelvin talked for hours about how miserable his marriage was. That it was a façade, and how he forced himself to smile in all the pictures. He said he was being controlled, and sometimes he was emotionally and physically abused by his wife. It was clear he needed someone to talk to, so I allowed him to vent and boast about his luxury cars, houses and businesses.

Kelvin called me every chance he could. Before long, he was telling me how much he liked me and wanted to see me. Even if I wanted to see him it was highly unlikely considering he lived on the West Coast. For me, it was nothing more than a way to pass time. We had fun talking about different genres of music, books and the many places he traveled.

He was totally different from anyone else. How we went from flirting on the phone to discussing marriage I don't know. But Kelvin was very adamant about us spending the rest of our lives together. "Joretta, I love you so much until it makes me cry." We had covered a lot over the phone, and I was very transparent with him about my life and what I had gone through. There was a lot of chemistry between us, and I needed to know it was real. Kelvin and I devised a plan on how we were going to merge our lives. He would file for divorce and move to Georgia. He started shipping anything that would fit in boxes to me. I received huge boxes of clothes, shoes and hats.

He told me he was going to leave all his cars and start over once he got here. One day he called me and told me he saw a BMW online he wanted. He said due to his pending divorce, he could not apply for any credit. He convinced me to go to the dealership and get the car in my name and he would pay it off. Love will make you do some stupid things. The car I had was paid off and the money I had saved was for a down payment on a house. I went to the dealership and the feeling in the pit of my stomach was so strong urging me not to do it.

Kelvin called, "did everything go through?"

"Kelvin, I'm trying to buy a house and if I get this car in my name it's going to mess up my debt-to-income ratio."

"Baby, I'm going to pay the car off in three months. I would prefer we buy a house together anyway so my name can be on it too. Once my divorce is final, I'm going to marry you and you won't have anything to worry about." At that moment, I would have purchased anything Kelvin told me to. I applied and got approved.

In January of the following year, Kelvin arrived. We were like two giddy teenagers when we saw each other. The first couple of weeks were great. By the third week, things started getting peculiar, I started getting calls from blocked numbers. He requested I get my number changed and delete my Facebook page. I also noticed he was taking a lot of medication. While he was in the shower, I looked in his bag and saw the medication he was prescribed was for schizophrenia, bipolar and manic depression.

Kelvin told me he never knew his biological mother. He said he was thirteen when his friends told him he was adopted. He confronted the lady who raised him, and she beat him and threatened to kill him if he ever asked her again. He'd heard stories from family members that the lady who raised him stole him from the hospital.

He said when it was time to get his learner's permit, he asked his mother for his birth certificate, but she didn't have one. She went to the department of vital records and made up a date of birth and paid the clerk for a fake birth certificate.

He said he knew then that she was not his birth mother. Kelvin cried and cried. He had tried on multiple failed occasions to find his birth mother and father. He said that he always wondered what his biological mother looked like and if he looked like her. Unfortunately, Kelvin would never know. He realized the older he got, the slimmer the chances were of finding his birth parents alive.

When it was time to make the first car payment, Kelvin didn't have the money. He left the next day and went back to the West Coast. After he left, I received a call from his daughter that they were worried about him because he told them he was going to visit his family for a couple of weeks. After they didn't hear from him, they had his phone tracked and checked his text messages and saw my number. She told me her father had been diagnosed with mental illness for quite some time. She stated he was having a manic episode when he left, and in his mind, the life he was going to start with me was very real.

I wanted to have sympathy for Kelvin, but I couldn't. What was the purpose of him coming that far to disrupt my life and leave me in financial ruin? What was it about me that keeps attracting these types of men?

Just give the Fuck up, Joretta! You're weak, you're stupid and you're broke. Nobody wants you. You don't even want you. You just need to kill yourself. The voices in my head were loud and clear. *God! Why am I here? Why God? Why didn't you give me any gifts? This Fucking Shit Hurts and I don't want to be here anymore! God, will you please take Bert or take me?!?!* I contemplated ways to kill myself. The closest I came was sitting in the car with the garage door closed waiting for the carbon monoxide to take me away. I probably would have been successful if it wasn't for a snicker bar I wanted to eat before I died. But once I went inside and ate it, I changed my mind. I needed some serious help. *You need to talk to Bert,* the voice said. You must give her the opportunity to tell her story. But I've tried and it hasn't worked.

I was over fifty when I had the conversation with Bert. She had stopped drinking for years and would probably be more receptive to talking to me. My first question to her was, "Bert, tell me about your childhood?"

She told me the story I had heard before of her biological mother leaving her with her paternal grandmother while she went to the store. She said, "my mother asked me what I wanted from the store. I told her a pack of shortbread cookies. I waited and waited, and I never saw the cookies or my mother again."

As she told the story, I could see the hurt of the little girl in her 83-year-old eyes. She said her paternal grandmother, Ms. Kate, whom she called mama, was very loving and took good care of her. When she was fourteen, she met a man in his late twenties. He was tall, dark, handsome, and fresh out of the military. She fell in love and at sixteen she had his baby. During that time, if a girl got pregnant, she had to drop out of school. Bert never completed the ninth grade and never returned to school.

Two years later, she was pregnant with her second child. A third child was born two years after that. I asked her, "Bert, if there was one thing you could have done what would it have been?"

Her eyes lit up and she cracked a half smile, and said, "I would have joined the Army."

"Okay, you would have made an excellent drill sergeant," I said. We both laughed.

I asked her about her relationship with Mr. Rutten and if she loved him. She said she did. She told me he loved to party and how handsome and well-dressed he was. She sounded like the little 14- year-old girl when she spoke of him. But she wasn't the only one who wanted him, and she wasn't the only one he wanted. After their relationship ended, she went on to have two more children with two different men (both babies were given up for adoption at birth to different families) before meeting my daddy, Howard.

Unlike Mr. Rutten who was smart and sophisticated, Howard was country and simple. She said when she got pregnant, Mama told Howard he had to marry her. Howard worked at the cotton mill, but he was irresponsible and unreliable. When the white man from the gas company came to turn the gas off, he saw she had a newborn baby and refused to turn it off. He also saw she didn't have a refrigerator and he got one for her. She said Howard drank constantly and beat her every time he got drunk, and when they went out, he encouraged her to drink too. She had four children to take care of so she couldn't work. She told me that every house we lived in, she was the one who found it and begged the landlord not to put us out when Howard didn't pay the rent. She said she found the last house we lived in before they abandoned me and my brother Shawn.

The owner was a man Howard used to work for. She said she had taken all that she could and couldn't take anymore. She never acquired any job skills, learned how to drive or dream. Being a man's pleasure and punching bag was all she knew. After hearing Bert's story, I felt relieved. I got it now, I understand. The anger and resentment I felt for her were gone. I had so much love for her. This lady had gone through so much and no one ever asked her how she was doing. I can't imagine what it was like for an uneducated Black woman growing up in a rural town in the south during the civil rights movement. I now had the answers I needed, a revelation. Before leaving, Bert said, "Jo, I got some fried chicken in there if you want some."

"You would offer me chicken now that I don't eat meat anymore," I said. We both laughed. And for the first time, I hugged her and said, "I love you, Mommy."

The men who came into my life was no accident. I was a damaged little girl, and they were damaged little boys. It's been said that a mother is the first woman a boy falls in love with, and if she breaks his heart, it's broken forever. Whether it was Michael, Clark, Matthew or Kelvin whose hearts were broken by their mothers, or Leon who dealt with the pressure of being his mother's favorite child but failed to live up to her expectations, they were as damaged as I was.

We were all suffering from trauma and projecting the pain and chaos onto each other. Until we heal that part of ourselves, we'll always be broken, damaged people looking for someone to put us back together. We will never be able to be whole until we forgive and love the person who broke us in the first place. Only then, can we genuinely love someone else.

All this time I was blaming Bert for my mistakes not realizing I had behaved the same way with my children. Minus the alcohol, I was just like her. I had modeled her behavior: down to her nervous tick of picking the skin off the heels of my feet until they bleed, biting my bottom lip and staring at the floor when I'm worried. Then there were the survival skills she taught me: improvisation, tenacity and grit. I had to have the conversation with Kee-Kee and allow her to express her anger and accept her telling me I was a great provider but a terrible mother for abusing her and forcing her to stay with the lady I trusted but violated her. Ashely and I reunited. After hearing my story, she forgave me for not keeping her and for the altercation we had. I've broken my son's heart and for that I am terribly sorry. Unfortunately, Jameal has not forgiven me, and we are estranged.

It is my sincere prayer that one day he will. I hope this book helps explain what I've been unable to explain all these years.

In 2022 I received my Bachelor of Arts Degree in English. I started doing the work on myself again: reading books about love and self-esteem. Today, I continue to practice yoga, healthy eating and deep breathing. I listen to good music, I laugh a lot and cry a lot, and I've surrounded myself with people who genuinely love me. But most of all, I have fallen so in LOVE with myself. As Dorothy Dix stated, "I do not regret the hardships I have known, because through them I have touched life at every point I have lived. And it was worth every price I had to pay. I can proudly say, I stood yesterday and today I am still standing!"

No One Knows

No one knows the real me

All the pain I feel inside Although I laugh and keep a smile The pain I try to hide.

No one knows the real me No, they can't even see the turmoil and the sadness That's felt inside of me.

Sometimes I often wonder When you look into my eyes Can you see what's going on? Behind the eyes that lies.

Can you see the loneliness? Can you see the hurt? No, because I hide it It's not easy, but it works.

Can you see the real me?

I find that hard to believe.

I know that I am a caring soul but still yet sometimes deceives.

The eyes are the window of the soul The heart controls the mind Maybe one day, I'll let someone in and the real ME, they will find.

Autor: Geraldine Benjamin. Hartsville, SC

Begin Again

For every up, there's a down for every lost, a win

For every rise, there is a fall for every foe, a friend

After sadness comes laughter After tears comes joy

For every man there's a woman for every child, a toy

So, if your day is not going well

And you feel you just can't win Remember, after night comes morning Get up! And Begin Again!

Author: Geraldine Benjamin. Hartsville, SC

ACKNOWLEDGEMENTS

Let us be grateful to the people who make us happy; they are the charming gardeners who make our souls bloom.

- Marcel Proust

- Bleach on Colored Clothes -

To my children, grandchildren, and great-grandchildren. Thank you for allowing me to be your mother, grandmother and great-grandmother. Thank you for your tolerance, understanding, patience and love. I love you more than you will ever know.

My Beautiful Sweet Niece Tambra: Where do I start? You have been on this journey with me from day one as my counselor and sounding board. Thank you for believing in me and standing with me and by me. Thank you for your love and light. Keep shining! Love you!

To K., my friend! You have been riding with me for over 25 years and have remained consistent. Your sense of humor and positivity have lifted me up from some of the darkest places. I truly appreciate your being supportive of everything I've wanted to do, no matter what it was.

Pamela B., my friend who is multi-talented, multi-faceted and a multitasker. We go back like a rewind cassette tape with a pencil. You have been a true friend. We can go for months without talking and pick up right where we left off. Thank you for meeting me where I was and being sincere. I love you.

Holly Rock! You have been my rock and my roll. Lol. Whether it's going to the Farmer's Market or on a road trip, you're packed and ready to go. Thank you for being such a good listener and friend.

Mrs. Lewis, my kindred spirit! I am so thankful for the day our paths crossed. You have been such a blessing to have as a friend. Thank you so much for giving me a safe space to be me. I Love You. Keep writing!

Deborah, a pastor once said, "God's answer to every problem is always a person." I thank God for you for opening your door to me and Kee-Kee when I had nowhere to go. Thank you for the times you made me laugh when I wanted to cry. Please keep writing. The world needs to hear your story. Love you much!

Nancy, you have been a big sister, employer, chef, teacher, spiritual advisor and friend. Thank you for giving me opportunities when no one else would. You have always believed in me even when I didn't believe in myself. Your enthusiasm is addictive. I love you for all you have done and for being You.

Ms. Annie!!!! I don't know what I would have done without you during those times when I felt like I couldn't go on. You have been a lifesaver (literally!) I will never forget that. I love you dearly.

To my editor and publisher Sarah Ratliff!!!! Wow! What can I say? You showed up and showed out. We met at the right place and at the right time. I can't thank you enough for your insight, intelligence, intellect, ingenuity, integrity and inspiration. Thank you for bringing this book to life. Thanks to my Bleach on Colored Clothes creative team, Sanja (cover and book designer), Grey (marketing) and Gwen (my website). I love the book trailer and everything you've all done for me. Thank you for your talent and creativity. I appreciate the time you spent making sure it was to my satisfaction. I am so grateful to have had the opportunity to work with all of you.

Thanks to my supporters Edward, Lee, Nancy, Deborah, B.O., Kim, Kamela and those whose names I did not mention. You know who you are.

Finally, to the one who always held me accountable. My Best Male Platonic (I made sure I mentioned platonic for those who thought we were more than friends), Friend and Brother from another mother. The late Reginald E. Arthur: you were so excited for me and always had my back. I could expect a call every week that always started with, "What Up! What Up! What Up!" in falsetto. And then, "What's up with the book?"

in your baritone voice. I miss you tremendously. You were indeed the best male friend any female could ask for and I am so thankful to say you were a friend of mind. I will hold onto the awesome memories and times we shared. Thank you for being a friend. I hope I made you smile. Love you forever and ever Reggie-Reg!!!! (1964-2019)

In Loving Memory of Clark December 2015 and Leon October 2020.

About the Author

Joretta King is a first-time author living in Atlanta, Georgia. Joretta is an avid reader of books about self-esteem, healing and love. She loves yoga, healthy eating and deep breathing. Apart from reading and being physically, emotionally and mentally healthy, the other love in Joretta's life is helping others heal. She loves giving therapeutic facials at Facials N Such.